含まれているのはチ…フレットと関連商品
日本の映画館から飛び出した
傑作や代表作の数々
漫画動画
宣伝貼札
芸術
犬夜叉
POCKET MONSTERS
ミュウツーの
劇場で待ってるよ!
同時上映
ピカチュウのなつやすみ
生きろ。
宮崎 駿 監督作品
ディエイチ出版社
ココロ
ブックス

Anime Poster Art

Published by DH Publishing Inc.
Address: 2-3-3F Kanda Jimbocho, Chiyoda-ku, Tokyo 101-0051
Japan
www.dhp-online.com

cocoro books is an imprint of DH Publishing Inc.

ISBN 0-9723124-4-7
Library of Congress Cataloging-in-Publication
Data is available
Printed in Hong Kong.

Producer: Hiroshi Yokoi
Publications Director: Clive Victor France
Design: Ichie Takahashi
Production: Tomokazu Nagai, Takako Aoyama, Tomoko Sakashita, Hiroko Harino
Photography: Hidetoshi Shimazaki
Special thanks to Patrick Macias,
Tetsuya Masuda (@Wonder www.atwonder.co.jp),
Katsuya Nakamura (Mandarake, Inc www.mandarake.co.jp)

Contents

Columns

INTRODUCTION

Journey to the West - Anime vs Cartoons

by Patrick Macias

Alakazam the Great (1960)
Sai yu ki

One of the greatest pop cultural blunders of the 20th century was the West's stubborn insistence that animation was, or had to be, "just for kids." While it has always been tempting to try and pin the blame on a certain Mouse That Shall Remain Nameless, this unfortunate perception was largely institutional in nature. The average citizen was expected to lap up the likes of *Huckleberry Hound* and *Chilly Willy* for the duration of their youth, and then reject animation outright until they sprouted children that could be used to perpetuate the next cycle, and so on. Any deviation from this socially approved path, such as watching "cartoons" past the expiration date, would usually result in one's peers branding them "an idiot," or worse.

Not only did these attitudes generate an incredible amount of guilt for adults who actually liked *Gilligan's Planet*, but they also had the unfortunate side effect of stunting the entire medium in the West (with a few sensational exceptions) at the level of "suitable for the whole family", i.e. "boring" and "no thanks" for the rest of us.

This probably would have gone on for an eternity had it not been for the fact that in the mid-1980s, young people around the world got hip to the fact that the animation they'd been watching was a) suddenly really good, and b) actually being made in Japan.

Those who connected the dots suddenly found themselves liberated from decades of badly animated bondage. It turned out that the medium could produce something more substantial than obnoxious woodpeckers, "wascally wabbits," and crass toy tie-ins. It could be made to deliver anything imaginable

People were suddenly encouraged to think of the maddest things they could. Giant robots with the strength of minor deities. Colossal space battleships staffed by wine-swilling pirates. Fetching alien girlfriends in tiger-print bikinis. Neo-Tokyo, already having exploded sometime before, was about to explode again. The odds are someone in Japan could either animate it, had done so already, or was currently in the process of feverishly storyboarding.

Toei Manga Festival (1978)
Toei Manga Matsuri

Toei Anime in the Early days

While word of this activity was shocking, such creative diversity was simply the way things were over there. Anime had been on Japanese television since the early sixties, but it had graced the big screen well before then, making an exceedingly official debut in 1945 with the propaganda film *Momotaro: Holy Solider of the Sea*; the Imperial Navy's only foray into both feature-length animation and cute little talking animals.

While significant anime films were released during the '50s and '60s, such as Osamu Tezuka's *Journey to the West* (AKA, *Alakazam the Great*), it wasn't really until the early seventies that anime movie-going became a major institution unto itself. Which is ironic given the fact that by this point, Japanese films had been largely abandoned by the masses. This was mainly because, as is still the case, tickets in Japan cost a hell of a lot of money, and secondly, you had to go to a big city just to be able to find a theater. It quickly became clear that it was a lot easier to simply stay home and watch television, which is precisely what many people were doing.

Be Forever Yamato (1980)
Yamato yo Towa ni

Except for during the summer holiday season when *Toei Manga Matsuri* hit. And when it did, every young Japanese person of elementary school age, whether boy or girl, was expected to attend. It was an epic-length anime film festival (not actually manga, despite the name) that would present as many as seven individual short subjects running the gamut from live-action super heroes, to aforementioned giant robots, to big-eyed girly romance, all the way to the headliner which usually was an adaptation of a classic fairy tale (You are now advised to contemplate the stunning poster for the 1978 model, when the bill was *Spider-Man*, *Captain Harlock*, *Candy Candy*, *Message From Space: Galactic Battle*, and *Puss in Boots*. That must have been a really good show.).

This sort of thing was, and still is, a very big deal. Owing to its once-a-year special event status, a comparison to Christmas wouldn't be far off the mark. And considering how rowdy the kids would get, kids who normally were busy setting the standards for good behavior so high you'd want to punish them, one might think the Shinjuku Koma theater had suddenly transformed into the Rialto on 42nd street.

Such an exciting occasion demanded a souvenir, and it came in the form of a full color program, or "pamphlet," sold in the lobby. A catalog of compelling characters, relationship flow charts, maps, detailed story synopsis, and creator/staff bios, these programs neatly summarized everything good and decent that Western animation was criminally lacking. Like attendance to the Manga Matsuri itself, its purchase was considered mandatory.

While very much a "for kids only" affair, the *Toei Manga Matsuri* was nevertheless an indoctrination rite of sorts; one that presented a holistic image of diversity in animation. This helped to create several generations of children who would not only grow up feeling perfectly comfortable going to the theater to see anime, but were also inclined to snap up the programs (it should be noted that Toei would often brazenly run trailers for their ultra-violent yakuza films during the Manga Matsuri, which created fans of an entirely different stripe).

Anime Theater Rush

Within a few years, the film industry caught on to the fact that they had a whole new audience to cater to. The runaway success of the *Space Battleship Yamato* movie in 1977, whose posters heralded the influential "Girl + Spaceship + Universe" school of design, gave studios and independent producers alike a shot of confidence. Pretty soon it wasn't only just the movie industry that was getting involved. Publishers like Kadokawa and record companies moved into the market and backed a host of new anime films. Legions of Japanese youths who might not have gone to the movies at all, except for Hollywood titles, were now supporting domestic product in the form of anime. 1979's *Galaxy Express 999* was the highest grossing film of the year. 1980's *Be Forever Yamato* very nearly trumped *The Empire Strikes Back*.

Urusei Yatsura 3: Remember my love (1985)
Urusei Yatsura 3: Remember my love

Predictably, science fiction was big at first. But by the mid-eighties, works as diverse as Rumiko Takahashi's genre-splicing comedy *Urusei Yatsura*, and the blatant sexuality and violence of *Golgo 13* (whose poster looks like it was advertising *Tron*, but no matter) had helped paved the way for the likes of 1992's *Porco Rosso*, a landmark work if only for the fact that pigs were now flying, and thus truly anything was possible.

Back in the States, relics from these anime movies transmitted a revolutionary message to those who managed to find them outside of Dai Nippon. That wasn't just a poster for *Harmageddon* or a program for *Mobile Suit Gundam III* mind you; they were signs that the status quo was not to be trusted and deserved to be toppled (Perhaps some might have preferred Mao, LSD, and fucking in the streets, but for Reagan/Thatcher-era latchkey kids, this was probably as good as it was going to get.). Like the Cargo Cults of the South Seas, who treated castaway items dropped from passing airplanes as holy objects, things which had been thrown together by advertising departments and marketing divisions were helping to ignite an almost religious fervor. Armed with 6th generation video copies of films meant to be seen in a theater, fans rushed into battle clutching posters and pamphlets, seeking to transform - well, if not the world - then at least the dominant perception of what animation could, and should be.

Then, and Now

Porco Rosso (1992)
Kurenai no Buta

Crazy as it might seem, it all came to pass. A couple of naughty tentacles and a few Hayao Miyazaki movies later, it is hard to find those who still hold on to antiquated notions that animation is fit only for either partially developed brains or purely for the Mouse-approved musical comedy format. And those that insist upon it are now routinely branded as "uncool" or worse.

In the wake of *Spirited Away*'s win for Best Animated Feature Film at the Academy Awards, one might think that the years of bitter struggle are finally over. Surely the future, illuminated by countless amusement park possibilities and lucrative co-productions to come, is positively atomic in its brightness.

Oh but if it were only so. Back in Japan anime is (like the rest of the country), well, not so much in dramatic decline, but in a serious holding pattern. Satellite and cable channels are increasingly clogged with new shows, but as with the directly marketed Original Video Animation, or OVA, this has frequently led more to shameless pandering than to consistently impressive work. The once mighty *Toei Manga Matsuri* has shrunk from a half-a-dozen heft to offering kids, usually all boys now, a paltry three short subjects. Successful anime features are now either Miyazaki titles (considered "for the whole family," interestingly enough) or fan-only affairs ... and even they couldn't figure out what *The End of Evangelion* was supposed to be on about.

Even as anime has finally become a globally recognized commodity, the form itself is no longer a cutting edge or attracting new talent (Heck, most of it is actually made in the Philippines and India nowadays.). Back in Japan, there's been a lot of flight, both on the part of creators and audiences alike, to video games and other media. A fusion of 2-D and digital imagery seems to be the future, but it's not easy for the veterans of the field to play catch-up. Meanwhile, the artisans who choose to do things the old-fashioned way risk turning into something resembling those anachronistic tofu makers that the department of education loves to makes documentaries about. And perhaps most frighteningly, thanks to those darn computers, live-action film can now routinely show audiences impossible mind-blowing things, the likes of which only anime and manga previously held a monopoly on.

Mobile Suit Gundam 3: Encounters in Space (1982)
Kidou Senshi Gundam

In short, everyone seems to have lost the plot. Before we start holding a wake, we should renew our vows. Have a walk down memory lane. Lord knows anyone who is affiliated with anime, be they a fan, an otaku, or someone in a marketing division, could probably use a decent history lesson right about now. Or at the very least a reminder of how great anime is when it is a mass medium with something to offer everyone, rather than strictly for kids only, for fans only, or a national treasure.

Wasn't that the whole point to begin with?

This missive should probably come not merely from the likes of long-winded essays (although those can be fun too), but from a dazzling full-color approach in which the entire evolution, from *Alakazam the Great* to *Pokemon*, is laid out with the dizzying peaks and valleys made gloriously manifest.

This book is then that indoctrination of diversity that you never got because old cartoons were always on. It is your own personal festival of anime. Let it take you wherever you want: to a hopelessly romanticized past or a brave new future. Now turn the page you lucky creatures.

- Patrick Macias is the author of the book *TokyoScope: The Japanese Cult Film Companion* (Cadence Books). A staff writer and editor for *ANIMERICA* magazine, he is also a freelance contributor to numerous international publications. His favorite anime feature film is *Adieu Galaxy Express 999* and his favorite short is *Porky in*

Harmagedon (1983)
Genma Taisen

Super Heroes

Brains, brawn and comfy boots

According to one recent ad, the prerequisites for a Super Hero are a) uncluttered cranium, b) attire, c) brawn, d) comfy boots, and e) strong bones. We beg to differ. Schoolboy sleuth Conan has little in the way of rippling muscles, but makes up for it with a head full of brains. Lupin may score with the chicks, but fails miserably in the fashion department. And although Street Fighter Ryu is undoubtedly strong-boned, he doesn't even possess a pair of boots. What makes a Super Hero? Turn the page and find out.

Cyborg 009: Legend of the Super Galaxy (1980, Toei)
Cyborg 009: Chou Ginga Densetsu
Director: Masayuki Akehi
Production: Toei Doga
130 min

Poster (20 x 29 inch) $10.00

Flyer (7 x 10 inch) $1.00

空前のアイデアと特撮映像で迫る壮大なスケールのスペクタクル・ロマン！
A story of unprecedented dimensions and never-seen-before computer imagery!

When an evil force threatens to unleash the ultimate power, only nine cyborgs stand between the destruction of the universe and the ending credits.

Locke the Superman (1984, Shochiku)
Chojin Locke
Director: Hiroshi Fukutomi
Production: Nippon Animation
119 min

Poster (20 x 29 inch) $10.00

緑の髪の超戦士 ロックー　撃て！魔女の千年王国を！
Locke, the green-haired super warrior! Smash goes the witch's 1000-year kingdom!

During a run of more than 30 years, Yuki Hijiri's manga appeared in numerous magazines before making it to the wide screen as a feature-length anime. Indestructible and ageless, the super-powerful Locke has few concerns besides battling witches and saving the planet.

Rumik World: Fire Tripper (1986, Shochiku Fuji)
Rumik World: Fire Tripper
Director: Motosuke Takahashi
Production: Shougakukan Production, Studio Pierrot
48 min

Poster (20 x 29 inch) $10.00

Adapted from the original story by Rumiko Takahashi, the action weaves between the modern day and the Era of Warring States. ***Fire Tripper*** is believed to be the forerunner of ***Inu-yasha***.

Lupin III: The Castle of Cagliostro (1979, Toho)
Lupin Sansei: Cagliostro no Shiro
Director: Hayao Miyazaki
Production: Tokyo Movie Shinsha
100 min

Poster (20 x 29 inch) $80.00

Program (8 x 11 inch) $18.00

巨大な城が動き始める！　影の軍団が襲ってくる！　生きては還れぬ謎の古城でついにめぐり逢った最強の敵！

An enormous castle begins to shake! Out of the shadows emerges an army!
No one gets out alive! In this mysterious castle dwells the toughest enemy of all!

Hayao Miyazaki's first feature-length anime for the silver screen. In a small European country, Lupin III et al rescue the beautiful Claris from the evil clutches of Count Cagliostro. A kind of James Bond meets Dick Dastardly.

Poster (20 x 29 inch) $18.00

Lupin III: Legend of the Gold of Babylon (1985, Toho)
Lupin Sansei: Babylon no Ougon Densetsu
Director: Seijun Suzuki, Shegetsugu Yoshida
Production: Toho, Nihon TV, Yomiuri TV, Tokyo Movie Shinsha
100 min

古代メソポタミアから……現代のニューヨークへ
バビロンの秘宝をめぐるエキサイティングな争奪戦！
From ancient Mesopotamia...to present day New York.
An exciting adventure in search of the hidden treasure of Babylon!

Lupin and gang travel to New York to hunt down the legendary golden tower of Babel. But they're not the only ones after the Babylonian treasure. Mean Mafiosa and aliens with a penchant for ancient civilizations also make appearances.

Lupin III: Dead or Alive (1996, Toho)
Lupin Sansei: Dead or Alive
Director: Monkey Punch
Production: Lupin III Committee
97 min

コイツは危険すぎる。
He's so dangerous.

Although the sixth feature in the Lupin III series, it was the first to be directed by the Lupin creator, Monkey Punch. Lupin's gang head to the despotic kingdom of Zufu in search of hidden treasure. It's when they manage to penetrate a prison island that their futures start looking a little less rosy.

Flyer (7 x 10 inch) $1.00

Akira (1988, Toho)
Akira
Director: Katsuhiro Otomo
Production: Akira Committee
124 min

Flyer (7 x 10 inch) $4.00

Poster of DVD (20 x 29 inch) $50.00

Program (8 x 11 inch) $30.00

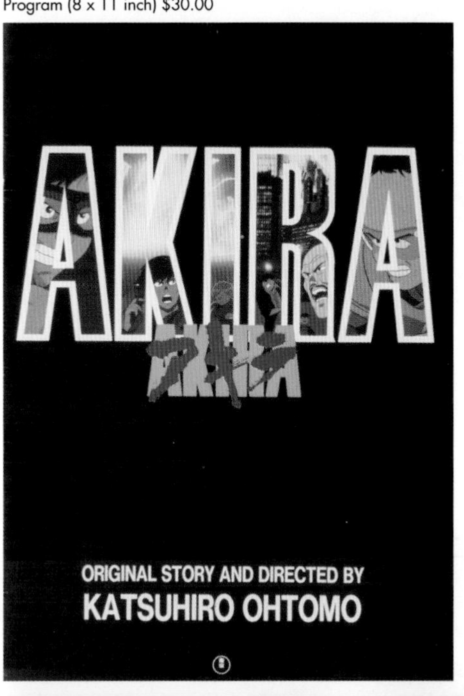

もう始まっている、もう止まらない…
It has started...and will never end.

Year: 2019 AD. Location: Post-World War III Neo-Tokyo. Plot: Government has a secret weapon in the form of Akira, a boy with special powers, who it uses in the war against an evil underworld gang. Heroes: Two street punks, Kaneda and Tetsuo.

For those who like a bit of data thrown into their anime soup, consider this: The two boys' full names are Kaneda Shotaro and Shima Tetsuo. In the classic anime TV series ***Tetsujin 28 Go***, the robot operator is a certain Kaneda Shotaro, while Shikishima Tetsuo is the son of the robot-inventing professor. And that's not all! In ***Akira***, Tetsuo's ID number is 28.
(BTW, Kaneda was born on September 5, 2003.)

Program (8 x 11 inch) $5.00

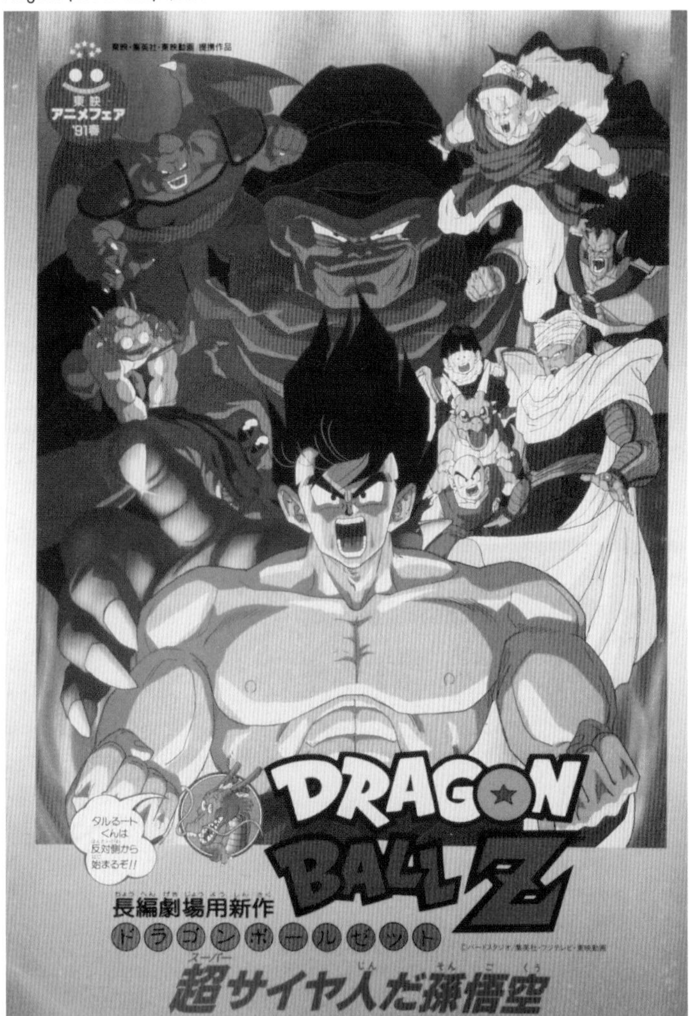

Dragon Ball Z: Lord Slug (1991, Toei)
Dragon Ball Z: Super Saiya-jin da! Son Goku
Director: Mitsuo Hashimoto
Production: Toei, Shueisha, Toei Doga
50 min

Slug, the Namek leader, has plans to take over the Universe. That's before Goku, Gohan and Piccolo step in. Although the title in Japanese is *Super Saiya-jin* (The Super Saiyan), in the original story Goku has yet to become a mighty Saiyan and therefore audiences expecting the big metamorphosis may be a tad disappointed. DBZ movies continued for years, taxing the abilities of the writers to create ever more villains that could be worked into the story.

Dragon Ball Z: The Return of Cooler (1992, Toei)
Dragon Ball Z: Gekitotsu!! 100 Oku Power no Senshi Tachi
Director: Daisuke Nishio
Production: Toei, Shueisha, Toei Doga
45 min

Program (8 x 11 inch) $3.00

In the previous episode, Goku destroys the cyborg Cooler. But now his brother, Frieza, has arrived and is itching for payback. Goku is more than happy to comply.

Program (8 x 11 inch) $3.00

Ultra-powerful Saiyan legend Brolly comes up against Earth's four toughest Super Saiyans: Goku, Vegeta, Future Trunks and Gohan. Warning: Contains fight scenes.

Dragon Ball Z: A Close battle, Violent Battle, Super Bloody Battle (1993, Toei)
Dragon Ball Z: Moetsukiro!! Nessen, Ressen, Chou Gekisen
Director: Shigeyasu Yamauchi
Production: Toei, Shueisha, Toei Doga
70 min

Dragon Ball Z: The Dangerous Pair! The Super Fighters Cannot Sleep (1994, Toei)
Dragon Ball Z: Kiken na Futari: Super Senshi wa Nemurenai
Director: Shigeyasu Yamauchi
Production: Toei, Shueisha, Toei Douga
50 min

Brolly returns from the dead to face the brothers Gohan and Goten, and Kid Trunks. In the last episode, Earth's toughest fighter, Kurillin, had given up after only 18 seconds. But this time Mr. Satan's daughter, Videl, goes a full two minutes without getting killed.

Program (8 x 11 inch) $3.00

Program (8 x 11 inch) $3.00

Dragon Ball Z: The Rebirth of Fuson! Goku and Vegeta (1995, Toei)
Dragon Ball Z: Fukkatsu no Fusion!! Goku to Vegeta
Director: Shigeyasu Yamauchi
Production: Toei, Shueisha, Toei Doga
51 min

The other world is inhabited by a red demon that changes itself into the vile Janemba. For Goku and Vegeta to stand a chance, they must fuse their power. This they do to become Gogeta.

Dragon Ball: The Road to the Strongest (1996, Toei)
Dragon Ball: Saikyou e no Michi
Director: Shigeyasu Yamauchi
Production: Shueisha, Fuji TV, Toei Doga
80 min

For the last feature-length ***Dragon Ball*** movie, the story returns to its roots. Bulma is searching for the seven Dragon Balls, which are believed to hold special powers, when she comes across a strange young boy named Goku. And the rest, as they say, is history.

Program (8 x 11 inch) $3.00

Yu Yu Hakusho: Poltergeist Report (1993, Toei)
Yu Yu Hakusho: Meikai Shitou hen Honoh no Kizuna
Director: Noriyuki Abe
Production: Shueisha, Fuji TV, Studio Pierrot
93 min

Poster (20 x 29 inch) $10.00

幽助より強い敵がいた！
A stronger foe than me!

In this sequel, Yusuke and his buddies come up against Yakumo, who, having destroyed the Spirit World, now has the human world in his sights. The two ghosts, Kurama and Hiei, became unlikely heart-throbs for a horde of adoring girl fans.

Flyer (7 x 10 inch) $1.00

Street Fighter II (1994, Toei)
Street Fighter II
Director: Gisaburo Sugii
Production: Capcom, Sony Music
101 min

超えられるか、俺を。
You reckon you can beat me?

Adapted for the big screen from the popular fight game, Street Fighter II pits all 16 characters in a battle of deception and strength. Will Chun-Li make it to the Academy Awards?

Spriggan (1998, Toho)
Spriggan
Director: Hirotsuge Kawasaki
Production: Spriggan Committee
90 min

戦って、死ね。
Fight, and die.

With the Earth's survival hanging in the balance, the heroes of this imaginative adventure are none other than a bunch of conservationists. Spriggan, a crack team of archeology buffs working under the auspices of ARCAM and led by super-scientist Yu Ominae, come across Noah's Ark. The discovery culminates in a Holy War with the role of anti-Christ played by - you guessed it - the evil Pentagon. Flyer illustrated by ***Akira*** creator, Katsuhiro Otomo.

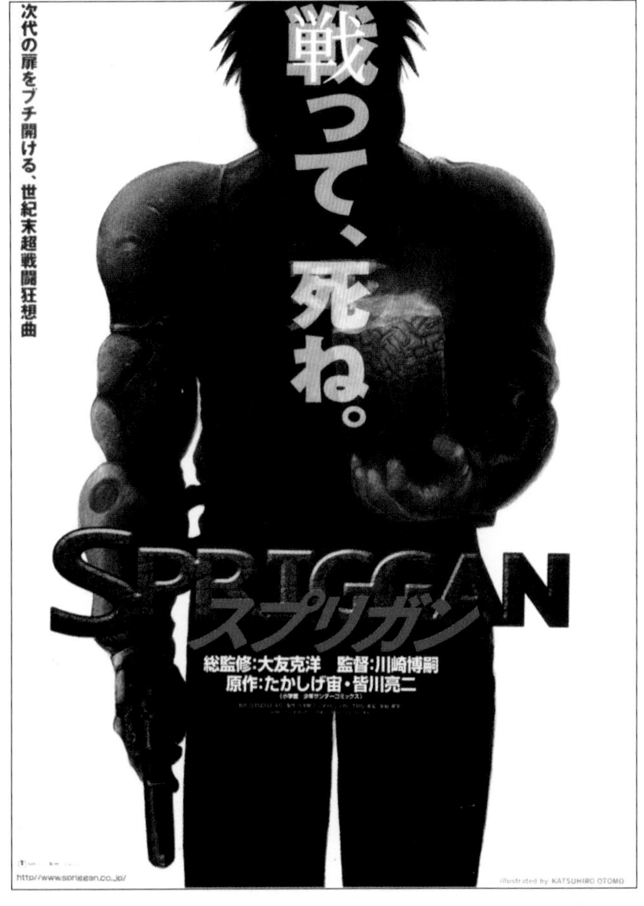

Flyer (7 x 10 inch) $1.00

Flyer (7 x 10 inch) $1.00

Detective Conan: Countdown to Heaven (2001, Toho)
Mei Tantei Conan: Tengoku e no Countdown
Director: Kenji Kodama
Production: Shogakukan, Yomiuri TV, Universal Music, Shogakukan Production, Toho, TMS
100 min

脱出不可能！　危険な罠の時間を止めろ。
No escape! Stop the clock ticking!

Japan's tallest building becomes the setting for a murderous game. Up against the evil society that changed him from Shinichi Kudo to boy-detective, Conan must survive and solve the riddle with the mysterious girl, Ai Haibara.

Flyer (7 x 10 inch) $1.00

Detective Conan: The Phantom of Baker Street (2002, Toho)
Mei Tantei Conan: Baker Street no Bourei
Director: Kenji Kodama
Production: Detective Conan Committee
107 min

夢か幻か!?　歴史の迷宮に隠された真実をつかめ！
Illusion or dream? Find the truth that lies hidden in the labyrinth of history!

A virtual reality game that combines the world's leading technologies is about to be released. At the unveiling ceremony, Conan joins 50 child contenders, and by doing so puts his life on the line. What ever happened to Space Invaders?

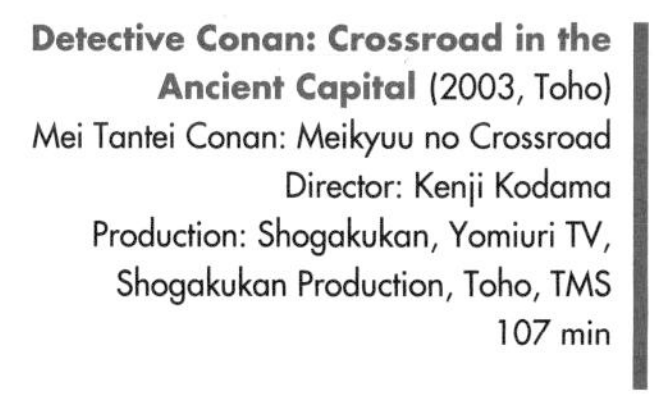
Detective Conan: Crossroad in the Ancient Capital (2003, Toho)
Mei Tantei Conan: Meikyuu no Crossroad
Director: Kenji Kodama
Production: Shogakukan, Yomiuri TV, Shogakukan Production, Toho, TMS
107 min

工藤新一、古都の謎に挑む!?
Shinichi Kudo, can he solve the mystery of the ancient city!?

One after another, five members of the crime gang Genji-Botaru are found murdered in Tokyo, Osaka and Kyoto. Conan and his rival, Heiji Hattori, set out to solve the crime. In what is a climactic ending to the series, Shinishi Kudo makes an appearance. But is he real or only a dream?

Flyer (7 x 10 inch) $1.00

Flyer (7 x 10 inch) $1.00

Inu-yasha: Love that Transcends Time (2001, Toho)
Inuyasha: Toki wo Koeru Omoi
Director: Toshiya Shinohara
Production: Shogakukan, Sunrise, Yomiuri TV Enterprise, Shogakukan Production, Toho, Nihon TV
100 min

ふたりの想いが新たな奇跡を呼ぶ
Two hearts together bring forth a new miracle.

Through a time-slip, high school girl Kagome Higurashi wakes up to find herself back in the Era of Warring States. There she meets Inu-yasha, a young half-demon who is battling the evil spirits that inhabit this long-ago world. Kagome gets caught up in Inu-yasha's quest to find and slay Menoumaru, his most formidable enemy. But, with trusty sword Tessaiga in hand, Inu-yasha must follow in his father footsteps, and ultimately fate tears the friends apart. A tear-jerker with lots of blood.

Inu-yasha: The Fantasy Castle Within the Mirror (2002, Toho)
Inuyasha: Kagami no Naka no Mugenjo
Director: Toshiya Shinohara
Production: Shogakukan, Sunrise, Yomiuri TV, Shogakukan Production, Toho, Nihon TV, Yomiuri TV Enterprise
99 min

宿敵・奈落との最終決戦！　そして恐るべき"かぐや姫伝説"の扉が開く。
The final battle against a sworn enemy, Naraku!
And the legend of the Princess Kaguya is revealed.

In this sequel, the evil Naraku somehow secures a piece of the smashed but still powerful Shikon Ball. With its energy released, it seems that even Inu-yasha and his cohorts have had it this time. No surprise to learn that yet another climactic Mother of All Battles is fought. However, one must wait till the end to find out if Inu-yasha's and Kagome's blossoming romance is crushed by the cruel hand of fate...

Flyer (7 x 10 inch) $1.00

One Piece: Adventure on Nejimaki Island (2001, Toei)
One Piece: Nejimaki Jima no Bouken
Director: Junji Shimizu
Production: Toei. Toei Animation, Shueisha, Fuji TV, Bandai
55 min

Flyer (7 x 10 inch) $1.00

あ"、仲間も船も、盗まれた!?
Oh no! Somebody's stolen my ship and all its crew!

Luffy has a dream that he's a pirate king, the only rationale necessary for him to set off in search of the legendary treasure known as One Piece. After his ship is pinched, Luffy and his band of hearty pirates finally reach Nejimaki Island. There they come face to face with the evil, all-powerful Trump, who lords over the island and his pirate followers. Readers of the manga bible, Shonen Jump, have made ***One Piece*** as big as ***Dragon Ball Z***.

Steam Boy (2004, Toho)
Steam Boy
Director: Katsuhiro Otomo
Production: Steam Boy Committee

Flyer (7 x 10 inch) $1.00

少年は [未来] を発明する。
A boy invents the future

Katsuhiro Otomo's first feature-length project since his breakthrough film ***Akira*** in 1988 cost a total of 200 million yen and took eight years to complete. The story takes place in 19th century England, the golden age of the steam engine. Boy inventor Ray gets caught up in an adventure to protect his grandfather Royde`s invention, the Steam Ball. But will the machine save mankind or lead to its downfall?

Poster Power

Give-away flyers now sell for the price of a small car

Film-related goods are big business. Just check out the toy racketeering that goes on under the guise of fast food. Posters and flyers, fortunately, are less mercenary. They exist to promote movies, and not the other way around. And, as advertisements, they have an inherent esthetic appeal that, however unintentional, makes them works of art. It's not surprising, therefore, that many have become collectors' items, commanding high prices and an elevated status in the world of movie memorabilia.

Priceless Promo

Japanese interest in cinematic spin-offs is a relatively recent phenomenon. It was only after World War II that such products were even viewed as anything but trimmings to be disposed of immediately the film left town. 25 years passed before Tokyo's numerous secondhand bookstores and junk shops began adding film leftovers to their already cluttered shelves. The '70s were also the time that many hobbyists made the leap from film-buffs to businessmen, launching movie memorabilia stores that now dot cities throughout the country.

The profusion of such stores is of little surprise when you consider the array of collectibles that the average film sucks into its orbit: programs, posters, flyers, press sheets, lobby cards, still photographs, cells, bromides, signs, books, magazines, ticket stubs, test film, promo goods, soundtracks, scripts, photo albums. Anything that has a whiff of celluloid has a potential buyer.

By sheer numbers, programs and flyers are top of the heap. The market for flyers - simple, one-sheet printed promos - continues to grow and ever greater amounts of yen change hands for what was once a throw-away item. First edition flyers for ***The Great Escape*** (1963) and ***A Fistful of Dollars*** (1964) can fetch 300,000 to 500,000 yen ($3,000 to $5,000). The same goes for the early James Bond, Steve McQueen and Alfred Hitchcock films, the flyers from which can be worth considerably more than their weight in gold. Interestingly, it is Western cinema that fuels the burgeoning Japanese market in movie-related goods.

Programs, those colorful paid-for souvenirs that we all take home from films and subsequently lose, are also highly sought after. Many that turn up on the shelves of stores are from dated flicks that have all but disappeared from circulation. Popular genres are SFX, such as ***Godzilla***, and horror: a young Christopher Lee as Dracula is sure to be snapped up with glee. Kurosawa is another who never goes out of fashion, with programs from his films selling from 100,000 to 150,000 yen each.

Anime Appeal

Anime pilots the Japanese image-culture machine today, and consequently its flyers and programs attract a lot of attention, especially overseas. Although demand in Japan has yet to exceed that for Western films, products from the early days of Toei Doga, such as ***Hakujya-Den*** (1958) and ***Sai Yu Ki*** (1960), can fetch tens of thousands of yen.

The rising star of Hayao Miyazaki has led to a sudden burst of market enthusiasm for anything that depicts one of his many creations. Flyers from ***Future Boy Conan*** (1979) and ***Lupin III: The Castle of Cagliostro*** (1979) are both coveted items, and promos from Miyazaki's early anime, such as ***Animal Treasure*** (Toei Doga 1971), are rare indeed. The market is still relatively young, and few anime flyers and programs exceed 5000 yen in price. But anyone with an eye for business already has it fixed on the not too distant future, when prices are sure to rise.

What the Japanese will pay for The Great Escape.

The Great Escape flyer $3,000

=

1. Average price of a small secondhand car (below 660 cc) **$3,200**
2. Fine for drunk driving or driving without a license **$3,000**
3. Average monthly salary of a 34-year-old car salesman **$3,120**
4. Price of 166 tickets to see a movie ($18.00 per adult) **$2,988**

*All prices are for Japan only

Leading Ladies

Grace, charm and kick-ass attitude

Leading ladies come in all shapes and guises: Cute little Sakura, devilish witch Lina, enchanting seductress Lum, ass-kicking A-Ko, and alien Ryoko are just a few of the many girls that have graced the anime screen. But whatever roles they play, these comic-book women bring to the movies a certain color and personality that no other characters can. Without our femmes fantasie, animation would be a dull world indeed.

Heidi, A Girl of the Alps (1979, Toho-Towa)
Alps no Shoujo Heidi
Director: Sumiko Nakao
Production: Zuiyo Enterprise
107 min

Flyer (7 x 10 inch) $1.00

とびこみなさい…世界中のひとびとの胸に!
Dive...into every heart!

Based on the Johanna Spyri classic, the film is a digest of the popular anime TV series. Set in the stunning scenery of the Alps, the story follows the carefree lives of two young girls, Heidi and her best friend Clara. The TV series was directed by Ghibli's Isao Takahata.

Urusei Yatsura: Only You (1983, Toho)
Urusei Yatsura: Only You
Director: Mamoru Oshii
Production: Kitty Film
80 min

Poster (20 x 29 inch) $20.00

Poster (20 x 29 inch) $20.00

宇宙を舞台にくり広げるトライアングルラブウォーズ！
Outer-space love-war triangle

Invitations to the wedding of Ataru Moroboshi and Elle have been sent out to the townsfolk of Tomobiki. And Lum, who's heard about it, is fuming. At the end, even outer space is aware of the wedding.

Poster (20 x 29 inch) $20.00

Urusei Yatsura 2: Beautiful Dreamer (1984, Toho)
Urusei Yatsura 2: Beautiful Dreamer
Director: Mamoru Oshii
Production: Kitty Film
98 min

<夢邪鬼の世界>から脱出なるか!!
Can we escape the world of dream demon Mujaki?!

When Mujaki the spirit-demon shows up at Tomobiki High School, things get weird. The school festival, planned for the following day, never arrives, as time appears to stop. Easily the most popular of the four UY productions.

Flyer (7 x 10 inch) $2.00

Urusei Yatsura 3: Remember My Love (1985, Toho)
Urusei Yatsura 3: Remember My Love
Director: Kazuo Yamazaki
Production: Kitty Film
90 min

ダーリン、忘れないで！うちのこと、忘れないで…
Do not forget me, oh my darling...

Half-pint wizard Lou entices Lum to Tomobiki's theme park Fairy Tale Land. There, he hopes to keep her through sorcery and trickery. Lacking the trademark slapstick humor, UY3 was a disappointment for many hard-core fans.

Urusei Yatsura 4: Lum the Forever (1986, Toho)
Urusei Yatsura 4: Lum the Forever
Director: Kazuo Yamazaki
Production: Kitty Film
95 min

Poster (20 x 29 inch) $10.00

Poster (20 x 29 inch) $10.00

ラムの角が消えた！友引町がうごめき始めた!
Lum's horns disappear! Tomobiki Town starts to squirm!

Ataru chops down the 300-year-old cherry tree belonging to the Mendo family. With the tree goes Lum's little horns and her extraterrestrial powers, and strange things start happening on the streets of Tomobiki. Lum fans loved the poster and hated the film. Even in the non-sensical world of anime a story has to make some sense.

Flyer (7 x 10 inch) $1.00

Oshin (1984, Toho-Towa)
Oshin
Director: Eiichi Yamamoto
Production: Sanrio Film
123 min

'84年は、おしんの春ー
1984 is springtime for Oshin.

The made-for-cinema feature based on the hugely popular TV series of the same name. The story revolves around the misfortunes of a young girl in pre-war Japan possessed of extraordinary strength. All parts are narrated by the original TV cast.

Project A-ko (1986, Shochiku-Fuji)
Project A-ko
Director: Katsuhiko Nishijima
Production: Soeishinsha
83 min

時代は今！天下無敵の女子高生!!
Your time is now! The invincible high school girl!

Slapstick comedy about a high school girl with superhuman powers and speed. The scene in which she lays waste to her town in an effort to get to school is superb. But it's not for everyone. Hayao Miyazaki called it, "that terrible anime where girls dress in school uniform and fire off machine guns."

Flyer (7 x 10 inch) $4.00

Poster (20 x 29 inch) $10.00

Himitsu no Akko-chan (1989, Toei)
Himitsu no Akko-chan
Director: Takashi Hisaoka
Production: Toei Doga
25 min

海だ！おばけだ!! 夏祭り
The ocean! The season of ghosts! Summer festival

When she opens her compact mirror and says the magic words, "Tekumaku Mayakon Tekumaku Mayakon", Akko has the power to change her shape. In this episode she chooses to become a seagull, Kappa and a white dragon. Not to be tried at home!

Chibi Maruko-chan: My Favorite Song (1992, Toho)
Chibi Maruko-chan: Watashi no Sukina Uta
Director: Yumiko Suda, Tsutomu Shibayama
Production: Sakura Production, Fuji TV
92 min

しみじみしましょう。
Let's take it easy.

Momoko Sakura created this wonderfully amusing tale of a little girl from the memories of her own childhood. Fueled by its catchy theme tune, the ***Chibi Maruko-chan*** anime spread like a virus, sparking a boom unprecedented in a country famed for its slavish trends. This is the second of the features.

Flyer (7 x 10 inch) $1.00

Flyer (7 x 10 inch) $1.50

悪党、魔族にモンスター
攻撃呪文でい～ちころだぁいっ！
Bad guys, demons and monsters.
Blast them all with my black magic flame!

Many times repackaged, ***Slayers*** made its big screen debut after appearing as manga, novel, game and music. Lina is a foxy, fun witch who, with her magic spells, does a lot of damage. Lina's part is narrated by anime's foremost voice actress, Megumi Hayashibara.

Slayers (1995, Toei)
Slayers
Director: Kazuo Yamazaki
Production: Slayers Committee
59 min

Flyer (7 x 10 inch) $1.00

Slayers: Return (1996, Toei)
Slayers: Return
Director: Kunihiko Yuyama
Production: Slayers Committee
60 min

最強の敵出現－リナ、ナーガ絶体絶命!?
The toughest foe yet! Is this the end of Lina and Naga?!

Lina and Naga meet a young girl who tells them that her village has been taken over by a secret society, and asks for their help. Lina remembers that the village hides an important secret, and decides to get stuck in. Naga finds it all a bit too hard to swallow...

Flyer (7 x 10 inch) $1.00

Slayers: Great (1997, Toei)
Slayers: Great
Director: Kunihiko Yuyama
Production: Slayers Committee
60 min

激突！リナvs.ナーガ。シリーズ最大の決戦か？
Lina and Naga clash! Could this be the biggest battle of the whole series?

After saving Workman Golem's daughter, Lina and Naga end up staying at her house. But when a power struggle leads to a proxy war, the two witches are pitted against each other in battle.

Slayers: Gorgeous (1998, Toei)
Slayers: Gorgeous
Director: Hiroshi Watanabe
Production: Slayers: Gorgeous Committee
62 min

魔法大決戦!!
Magic Decisive Battle!!

Lina and Naga suddenly find themselves having to defend a bustling market town against an attack by a dragon army. But the leader of the army is none other than the daughter of the feudal lord. And her reason for such drastic action is over what she deems insufficient pocket money. The altercation between child and father has split the family down the middle. And Lina and Naga are also divided. Lina takes the side of the penny-pinching father. Naga joins with the demanding daughter. And again, the two friends look set to come to blows.

Flyer (7 x 10 inch) $1.00

Flyer (7 x 10 inch) $2.00

Tenchi Muyo in Love (1996, Gaga Communications)
Tenchi Muyo in Love
Director: Hiroshi Negishi
Production: Tenchi Muyo the Movie Committee
94 min

過去に問題　あ・り!?
Problem in the past?

Due to a mistake in the revolving axis of Time, Tenchi Masaki begins to disappear. To put a stop to this inconvenience, Tenchi travels back in time, where he meets a beautiful girl. Only later does he discover that she is in fact his very own mother, who died while he was still young.

Tenchi Muyo: Midsummer's Eve (1997, Toei)
Tenchi Muyo: Manatsu no Eve
Director: Satoshi Kimura
Production: Tenchi Muyo: Midsummer's Eve Committee
60 min

パパ、会いたかった！
Daddy, I missed you!

A girl turns up claiming to be Tenchi's daughter, and the Masaki household is thrown into panic. But lurking in the background is a shadowy figure that hold's a grudge against Tenchi's grandfather.

Flyer (7 x 10 inch) $2.00

Flyer (7 x 10 inch) $2.00

Tenchi Muyo in Love 2 (1999, Gaga Communications)
Tenchi Muyo in Love 2: Harukanaru Omoi
Director: Hiroshi Negishi
Production: Tenchi Muyo in Love 2 Committee
95 min

川のへの　つらつら椿　つらつらに　見れども飽かず　巨勢の春野は
[Kawa no e no/Tsuratsura tsubaki/Tsuratsura ni/Mire domo akazu/Kyosei no haruno wa]

When Tenchi suddenly disappears, his two rival girlfriends go in search of him. But when they find where he is, they discover he has lost his memory and is living with another woman. How inconsiderate, and they've come all that way...

Nadesico The Movie: The Prince of Darkness (1998, Toei)
Kidou Senkan Nadesico: The Prince of Darkness
Director: Tatsuo Sato
Production: Nadesico Committee
80 min

光を超えて、届けこの想い
Cross over the light, and send my love

To prevent a coup d'etat against mankind itself, 16-year-old Ruri Hoshino once again sets sail aboard the good ship Nadesico. Ruri was made lead in the film to silence the die-hards, who were baying for blood.

Flyer (7 x 10 inch) $1.00

Revolutionary Girl Utena the Movie (1999, Toei)
Shoujo Kakumei Utena: Adolescence Mokushiroku
Director: Kunihiko Ikuhara
Production: Revolutionary Girl Utena Committee
85 min

Flyer (7 x 10 inch) $5.00

もうひとりの僕よ、世界を革命する力を我に
This is the other me. Give me the power to change the world

When the pretty young boy Utena Tenjou is transferred to a new school, no one realizes that she's actually a girl in disguise. And it just gets weirder. She becomes engaged to a quiet young thing called Rose Bride, and is romanced by a gorgeous young fellow student. She has the power to change the world, but is unsure how it should be used. Based on a beautifully drawn *shojo* manga, the original TV series, replete with mysterious storyline and haunting choral score, quickly became a cult show beyond the confines of anime. The film version introduces a very new story with yet-to-be-seen characters.

Card Captor Sakura the Movie (2000, Shochiku)
Card Captor Sakura
Director: Morio Asaka
Production: Bandai Visual, Shelty, Madhouse
82 min

Flyer (7 x 10 inch) $1.00

香港を舞台にさくらの魔法が封印解除!!
It's in Hong Kong that Sakura's magic is released!

Sakura Kinomoto wins a trip to Hong Kong in a local raffle. But on her first night there she suddenly awakens after dreaming of a great wizard. Was this trip really just luck, or has it all been planned? CCS is big with cosplayers, and adult males who can't help themselves.

Flyer (7 x 10 inch) $2.00

Ah! My Goddess (2000, Shochiku)
Ah! Megami-sama
Director: Hiroaki Aida
Production: Ah! My Goddess Committee
105 min

ボクは君を忘れない
I'll never forget you

Keiichi Morisato is a Nekomi Tech University student with a secret. Together with Belldandy, she's a goddess living in the human world. They both join the school car club and attend a party to welcome new members. There, Keiichi is approached by a junior emboldened by booze. But just at that moment bottles start to explode and glasses shatter into tiny pieces. Why is Belldandy using her special powers? What can it all mean? And who will pay for the next drinks?

Millennium Actress (2002, Klock Worx)
Sennen Joyuu
Director: Satoshi Kon
Production: Millennium Actress Committee
87 min

千年かけても逢いたい人がいます
I want to meet him, even if it takes 1000 years

Chiyoko Fujishima, once the world's greatest actress, discovers an old key that unlocks a 1000-year life of happiness and grief, and remarkable adventures. Satoshi Kon is better known for his anime classic, ***Perfect Blue.***

Flyer (7 x 10 inch) $1.00

In the Marketplace

The biggest grossing anime in Japan?

On opening nights, adults unabashedly line up outside theaters to catch the latest anime releases. The boundary that once separated children and grownup viewers has long disappeared. As business and as entertainment, animated films are firmly established in the Japanese psyche as both a major industry and a cultural asset.

Anime comes to town

Farewell to Space Battleship Yamato was the first anime to make it to the annual ranking of Japan's top ten domestic films. Influenced by the televised series, that became a runaway success in 1977, the wide-screen version hit the number 5 slot the following year. The story, which blends human pathos with mechanical might, drew avid fans to theaters countrywide. A year later it was Hayao Miyazaki's turn, when ***Lupin III: The Castle of Cagliostro*** bewitched moviegoers of all stripes. The two films reshaped the skyline of motion pictures, and would leave an indelible mark on Japanese society.

By the end of the 1950s, Toei Doga was already producing commercial anime. However, its limited fare was overshadowed by grander projects. ***Godzilla*** was successfully stomping his way through Japan's on-screen urban clutter, and Akira Kurosawa was producing one mesmerizing hit after another. Anime was mostly limited to seasonal events, such as Toei's Manga Festival and Toho's Champion Matsuri, both screened during the long school holidays of Obon and spring. It was only at the end of the '70s, following the boom of anime and manga in other media, that feature-length animation began to flourish.

The advent of the television brought immediate change to viewing patterns and, unsurprisingly, it was cinema that lost out. However, for anime, the small screen offered the ideal stage and its popularity soared. By this circuitous route, anime returned to the movie houses, but by this time it had attained a standing far above its made-for-kids precursors. Still, due to those early festivals, it has never been able to entirely shrug off it juvenile image.

The anime industry

Studio Ghibli's recent successes have brought international fame and repute to its founders, Hayao Miyazaki and Isao Takahata, and its productions continue to outsell non-anime, Western and Japanese alike. However, the two have spent years honing their talents on masterpieces of animated cinema that reached out to fans of all ages. Studio Ghibli, having surpassed even Disney, will undoubtedly continue to produce anime of high quality, and their films and those of others in the industry may soon monopolize the coveted top ten slots. Proof, if still required, of this surge in popularity is the Academy Award-winning ***Spirited Away***.

As with Ghibli's productions, anime, such as ***Pokemon*** and ***Detective Conan***, share another common feature: there success is not limited to film. TV series, character goods, games and videos are just a few of the many ways anime is being remarketed on a huge scale. The medium offers unprecedented scope for repackaging. The ubiquity of spin-offs in Japanese society simply emphasizes the extent to which anime has penetrated the nation's culture. Entertainment in the form of film is now only one of many anime categories. In this fertile environment, quality and production can only increase.

Spirited Away - Who got what of the $300 million takings.

***Spirited Away* accounted for 15 percent of Japan's overall box-office takings of 2001. Although created by Studio Ghibli, another five companies invested in the film, with Toho acting as distributor. Where the box-office earnings of $300 million ended up can be seen in the chart below. 50 percent was divided up amongst the six investors. However, it followed a route different to most Japanese films, where the distributor then receives 20 percent. With Hayao Miyazaki's name guaranteeing success, Toho generously accepted 10 percent and the remainder was passed on to investors. But even with such sums being made, it is telling that Miyazaki's tax declaration for 2002 was a mere $250,000.**

Japan's Top Grossing Anime

Rank	Title	Box-Office Takings ($ million)	Release Date
1	Spirited Away	300	2001/7
2	Princess Mononoke	113	1997/7
3	The Cat Returns	65	2002/7
4	Pokemon: Spell of the Unown	48.5	2000/7
5	Pokemon: Mewtwo Returns	41.5	1998/7
6	Pokemon: Celebi: A Timeless Encounter	39	2001/7
7	Pokemon: Revelation Lugia	35	1999/7
8	Detective Conan: The Phantom of Baker Street	33	2001/2
9	Doraemon: Nobita and the Legend of the Sun King	30.5	2000/3
10	One Piece: Adventure on Nejimaki Island	30	2001/3
11	Doraemon: Nobita's Winged Heroes	30	2001/3
12	Detective Conan: Countdown to Heaven	29	2001/4
13	Porco Rosso	27.6	1992/7
14	Pokemon: Guardian Spirits of the Water Capital: Latias and Latios	27	2002/7
15	Pom Poko	26.3	1994/7
16	Tottoko Hamutaro: Hamuhamu Land Adventure	26	2001/12
17	Detective Conan: Captured In Her Eyes	25	2000/4
18	Doraemon: Nobita and the Robot Kingdom	23	2002/3
19	Kiki's Delivery Service	21.5	1989/7
20	Farewell to Space Battleship Yamato: In the Name of Love	21.2	1978/8

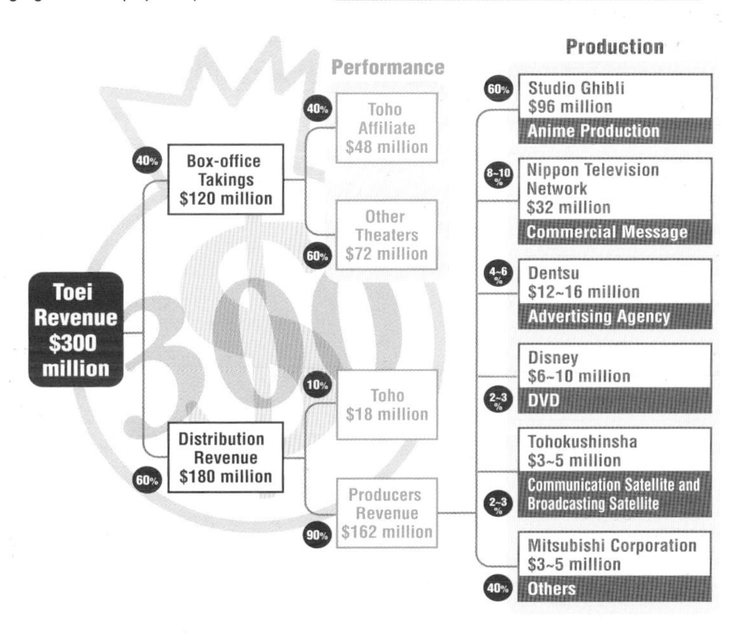

Robot Wars

Mega-weapons and death metal

Built with the most advanced technologies known to animated man, robots serve but one purpose: To kick butt! And, in the future worlds that these anime portray, there's a lot of butt to kick. Just watch Mobile Suit Gundam. When it's not laying waste to the environment, or trampling buildings a la Godzilla, it's flying through space blasting mega-weapons at anything that dares to blink.

The Ideon (1982, Shochiku)
Densetsu Kyoshin Ideon
Director: Yoshiyuki Tomino
Production: Nippon Sunrise
182 min

Poster (20 x 29 inch) $30.00

Flyer (7 x 10 inch) $3.00

異なる文明が不幸な出会いをした。誤解が死を呼び、傷口が広がっていく…
The meeting of two civilizations was ill-fated. Misunderstanding leads to death, injury becomes widespread...

Although the premise of this film, a war between humans and aliens, set the tone for numerous anime to come, ***The Ideon*** came to a close after 39 TV episodes, four short of the planned 43. To satisfy the hunger of die-hard fans, two feature films, entitled ***Hatsudou-hen*** (The Effect), were made. At the core is the edited collection of the TV series, ***Sesshoku-hen*** (The Contact), and the remaining four episodes that never made it to the small screen.

Mobile Suit Gundam (1981, Shochiku)
Kidou Senshi Gundam
Director: Yoshiyuki Tomino
Production: Nippon Sunrise
137 min

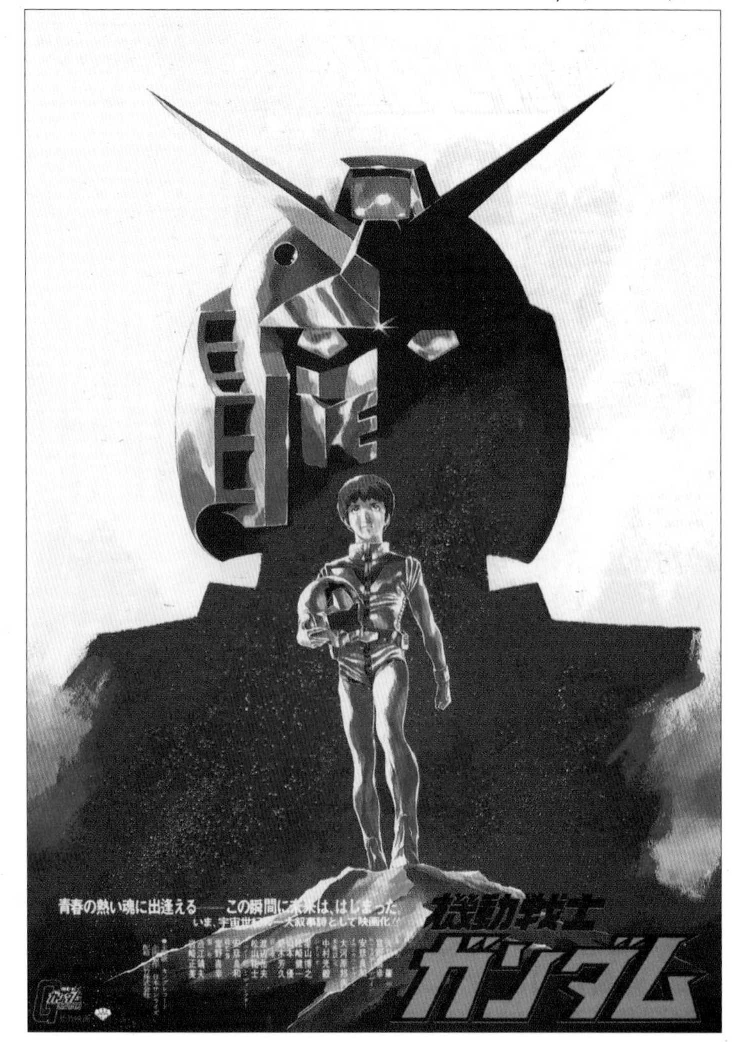

Flyer (7 x 10 inch) $4.00

青春の熱い魂に出逢えるーこの瞬間に未来は、はじまった。
I met a young man full of life, and at that moment the future began.

The first of three movie house films adapted from the TV series digest of 43 episodes. Based in outer space, the story follows the development of Gundam pilot Ray Amuro. ***Mobile Suit Gundam*** is recognized as the masterpiece of robot anime, and even now a new series is being created.

Mobile Suit Gundam III: Encounters in Space (1982, Shochiku)
Kidou Senshi Gundam III: Meguriai Sora
Director: Yoshiyuki Tomino
Production: Nippon Sunrise
141 min

Flyer (7 x 10 inch) $4.00

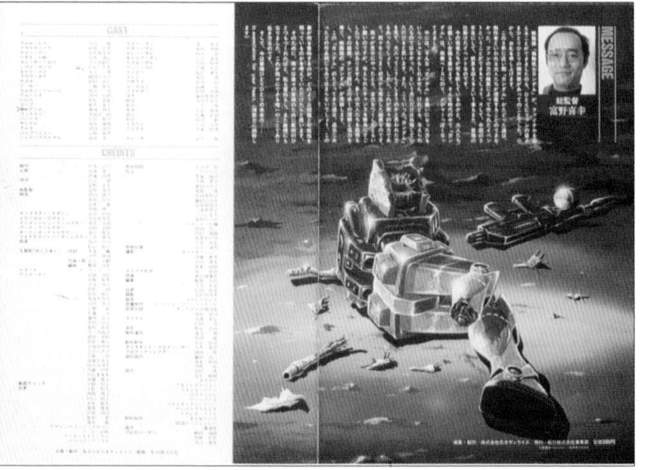

Program (8 x 11 inch) $6.00

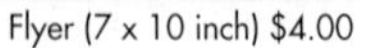

震えるか宇宙　めぐりあえよ生命
Space reverberates - Souls meet by chance

In the third film of the series, the Zeon space fortress A Baoa Qu amasses its forces against The Earth Federation and so unleashes the war to end all wars. Sound familiar? Gundam fans will enjoy the plethora of inter-character plots as old scores are settled and new allies team up.

Flyer (7 x 10 inch) $1.00

Mobile Suit Gundam F91 (1991, Shochiku)
Kidou Senshi Gundam F91
Director: Yoshiyuki Tomino
Production: Sunrise
115 min

目覚めよ宇宙。"ガンダム" 新時代ー第一章
Space, awaken! The New Era of Gundam, Chapter 1

Produced by staff members of the original TV series, who know a good thing when they see it. The Earth Federation meets the reformist group CrossBone Vanguard in a battle that revolves mostly around the film's hero, Seabook Arno. Minutes of celluloid are given over to never-before-seen familial interrelations, which may prove disturbing to fans expecting two hours of violence.

Gundam the Movie (1998, Shochiku)
Gundam the Movie
Director: Yasunao Aoki, Mitsuko Kase, Takeyuki Kanda, Umanosuke Iida
Production: Sunrise
140 min

ふたつの「G」が立ち上がるー。
The two Gs arise -.

A double feature to celebrate Gundam's 20th birthday. ***Gundam Wing: Endless Waltz*** and ***Gundam: MS 08 Team: Miller's Report***. With Boy Bands filling the charts, ***Gundam Wing***, which features five teenage lads, was made with female fans in mind.

Flyer (7 x 10 inch) $1.00

Flyer (7 x 10 inch) $3.00

Fang of the Sun Dougram (1983, Shochiku)
Document: Taiyou no Kiba Dougram
Director: Ryosuke Takahashi
Production: Nippon Sunrise
80 min

真実は見えるか…
Can you see the truth?

On a faraway planet, the locals have had enough of being a colony of Earth, and launch an independence movement. Although the unlikely named Crinn Cashim is son of the Head of the Federation Council, he's not big on the colonists. This he demonstrates by piloting a Dougram, the mobile armor that has come to symbolize the pro-independence forces.

Xabungle Graffiti (1983, Shochiku)
Xabungle Graffiti
Director: Yoshiyuki Tomino
Production: Nippon Sunrise
84 min

君は走るか、俺たちゃ走る！
Will you run? We will!

Earth is known as Planet Zora and Jiron Amos wants payback. Timp Shalloon killed his parents and he's been after him ever since. But when Jiron decides to steal a Xabungle Walker-Machine things start to heat up. The film is made up of the best cuts from the 50 made-for-TV episodes.

Poster (20 x 29 inch) $10.00

The Super Dimension Fortress Macross: Do You Remember Love? (1984, Toho)
Chou Jikuu Yousai Macross: Ai Oboete Imasu Ka
Director: Noboru Ishiguro, Shouji Kawasaki
Production: Bigwest
115 min

Flyer (7 x 10 inch) $1.00

ミンメイ　最大戦速!!
Minmay at Macross-speed!!

Way out in deep space floats Macross, a fortress-ship that has lost its ability to return to Earth. With the future of mankind at stake, Macross resident Hikaru Ichijo fuses his transformable jet fighter Valkyrie with the voice of singer Lynn Minmey to produce a formidable though rather unorthodox weapon. With this they fight yet another apocalyptic battle. Although there are numerous ***Macross*** series, all invariably feature a love triangle, the fighter Valkyrie and a voice-weapon.

Armored Trooper Votoms (1985, Shochiku)
Soukou Kihei Votoms
Director: Ryosuke Takahashi
Production: Nippon Sunrise
53 min

Poster (20 x 29 inch) $10.00

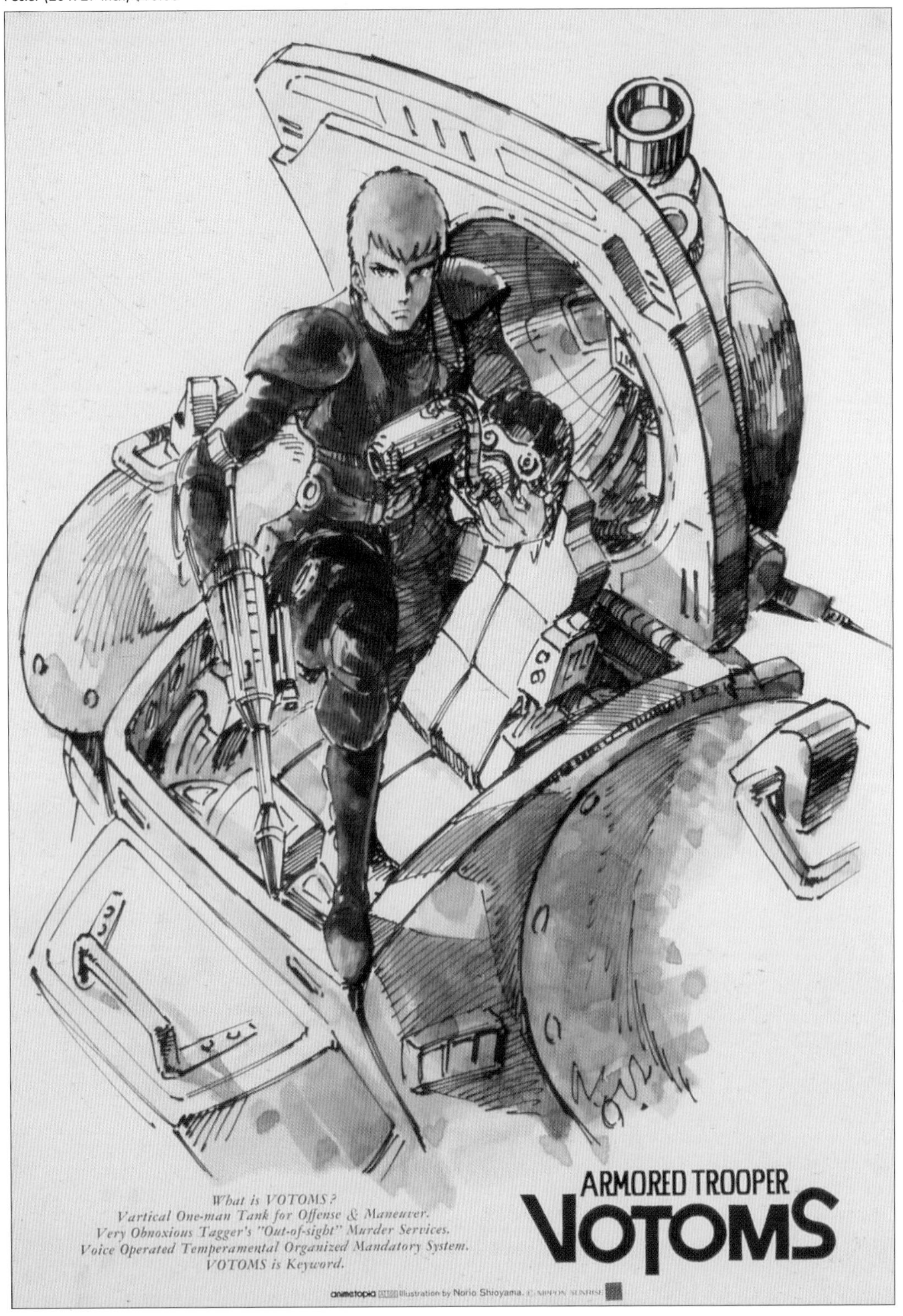

A 100-years war rages. No one remembers how it began, but the combatants are four-meter tall mass-produced robots, known as Armored Troopers, that are used up and discarded with comparative ease. Our hero, Chirico Cuvie, who pilots an Armored Trooper, has been fighting for so long he's forgotten what it's like to feel human. Character design by artwork superhero Norio Shioyama.

Poster (20 x 29 inch) $18.00

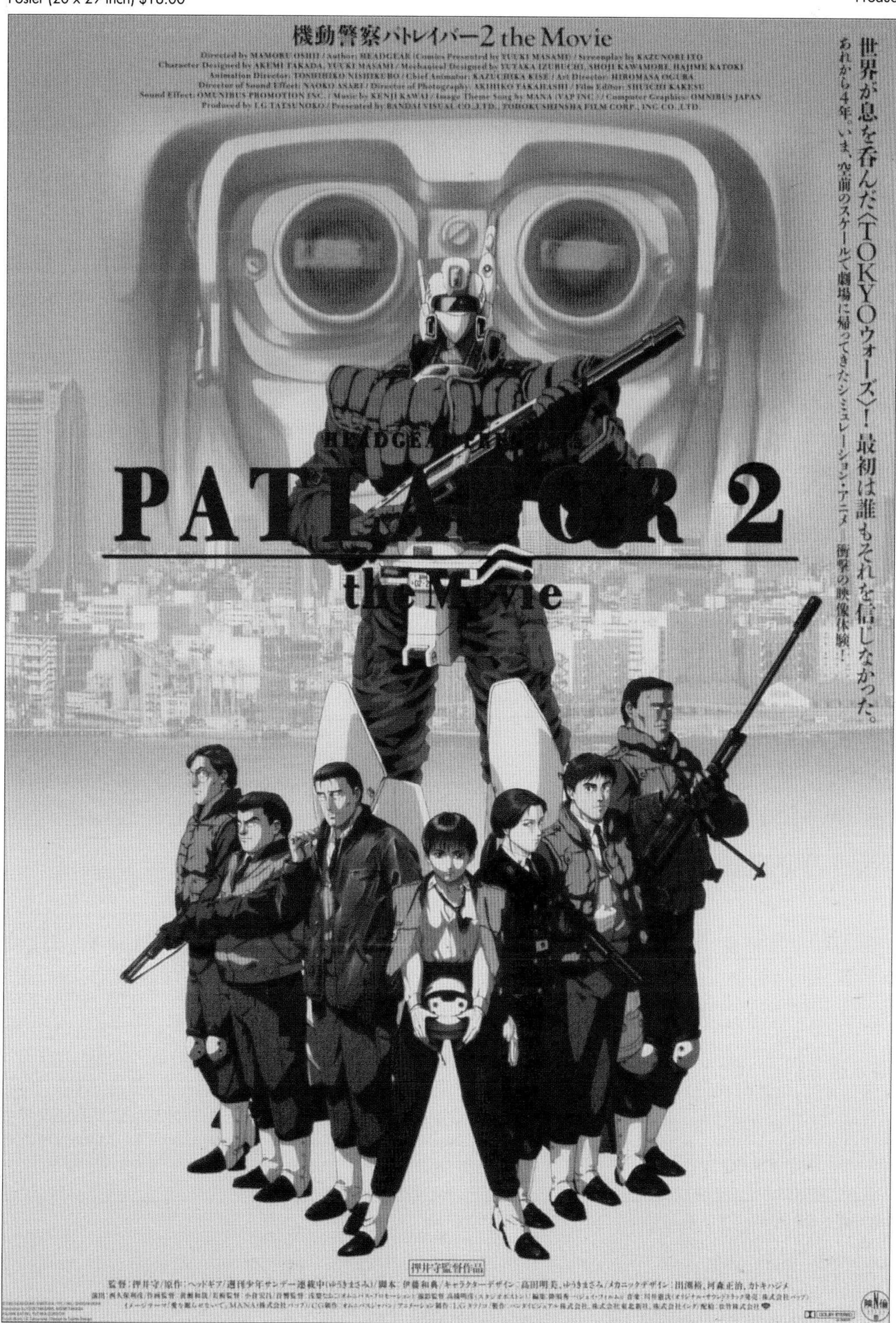

世界が息を呑んだ<TOKYOウォーズ>！最初は誰もそれを信じなかった。
TOKYO WARS will take you breath away! No one believed it could happen.

In the Tokyo of the future Patlabor are piloted by the officers of Special Vehicle Section 2, a police division that controls the illegal use of human-shaped worker robots known as Labor. Noah Izumi, a star Patlabor Ingram 98 Series Type 1 pilot, takes on a powerful enemy whose plan is to take over the government. George Bush, beware!

Flyer (7 x 10 inch) $1.00

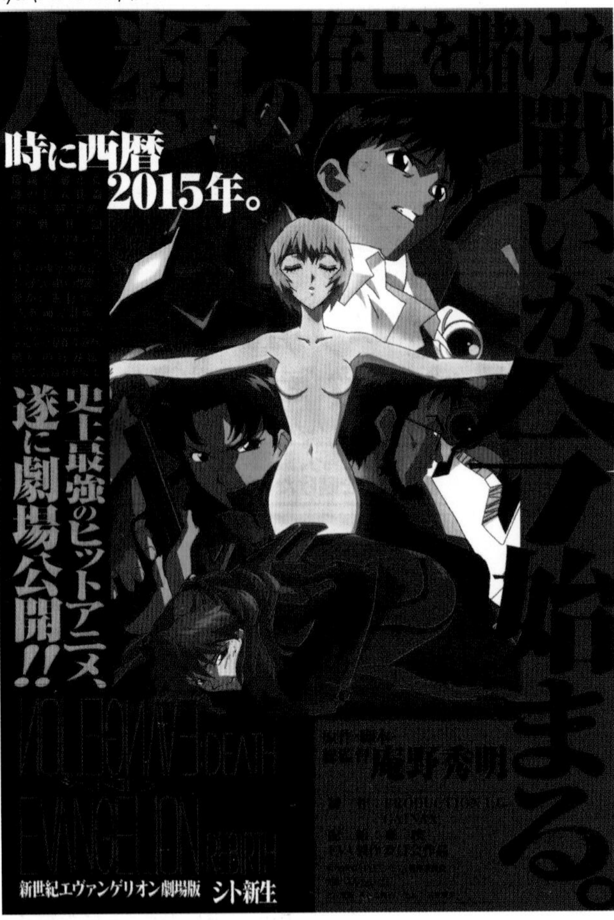

Neon Genesis Evangelion: Death and Rebirth (1997, Toei)
Shinseiki Evangelion: Shito Shinsei
Director: Hideaki Anno
Production: EVE Committee
99 min

人類の存亡を賭けた戦いが、今始まる。
Mankind's battle for survival is about to begin.

In 2015, following Second Impact, an unexplained disaster on Earth, the few survivors are visited by mysterious forces known as Angels. On the day the Angels appear, Shinji Ikari is visiting his father at the Special Institute NERV. It is the first time they have met in 10 years, and Shinji is surprised to hear what his father has to say. "Take control of Evangelion and destroy the Angels!" he tells his son. And thus begins the great battle for mankind's survival.

Flyer (7 x 10 inch) $1.00

Neon Genesis Evangelion: Death (True)2/Air/My Pure Heart for You
(1998, Toei)
Shinseiki Evangelion: Death (True) 2/Air/Magokoro wo Kimi ni
Director: Hideaki Anno
Production: EVE Committee
155 min

Poster (20 x 29 inch) $10.00

Program (8 x 11 inch) $6.00

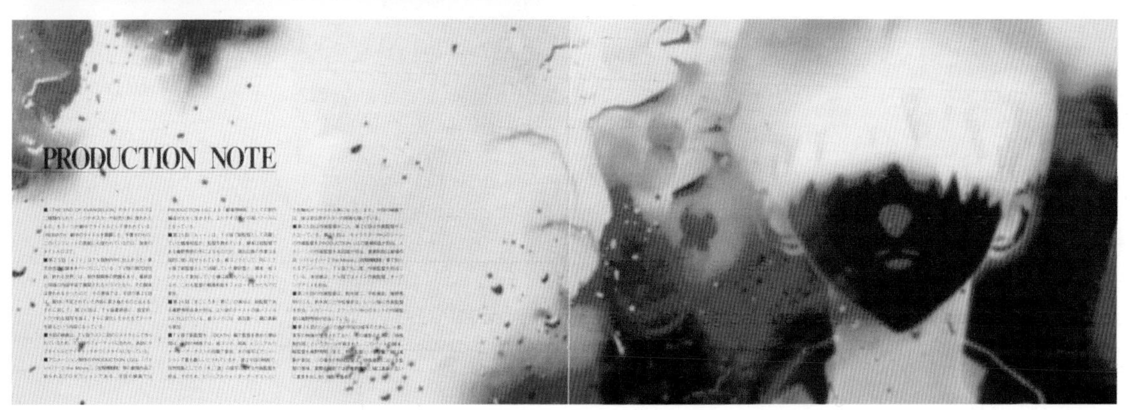

Death is a digest of the first 24 TV episodes

Rebirth leads the film away from the TV series.

Air/My Pure Heart for You is a psychological drama that combines the original plot with the TV episodes 25 and 26, which have little in common with previous programs.

Escaflowne (2000, Omega Project)
Escaflowne
Director: Kazuki Akane
Production: Sunrise, Bandai Visual
95 min

Poster (20 x 29 inch) $10.00

バァン、あなたは いつも、ひとりで戦ってるー。
Bahn, you are always fighting alone - .

School girl Hitomi has lost her will to live. That is until she meets Bahn, a boy from another dimension. Together, they return to his world for fun and games. Although a remake of the TV series, the film features a whole new story and design, which has led to a fan revival. Maaya Sakamoto, who does the voice of Hitomi, has also found fame as the singer of the film's theme song, Ring.

Rahxephon (2003, Shochiku)
Rahxephon: Tagen Hensou Kyoku
Director: Yutaka Izubuchi
Production: Media Factory, Victor Entertainment, Bones, Fuji TV, Shochiku
120 min

Flyer (7 x 10 inch) $1.00

怖れるな我が半神よ、汝の全ては私と共に…
Do not fear, my brother, we are in this together...

Mu, an alien from another dimension, turns up in Japan and decides on a whim to enclose Tokyo in a dome-shaped force field. Three years later, Ayato Kamina, who is still diligently attending school, meets a young woman who says she can help him escape. What he doesn't realize is that she is his past girlfriend, but living outside the dome she has aged 12 years while he has only aged by three. Sounds like something concocted by the lunatic fringe at the Immigration Dept.

Spaced Out

Anime, the final frontier

Sci-Fi anime boldly goes where no cartoon has been before. Which means you don't have to hang around waiting for aliens to visit Earth. Simply hitch a ride with Space Battleship Yamato and you'll be at the far reaches of the universe in under 10 minutes. Alternatively, board the next departing Galaxy Express 999 for a quick tour of the Solar System, and be back in time for dinner.

Flyer (7 x 10 inch) $4.00

Galaxy Express 999 (1979, Toei)
Ginga Testudo 999
Director: Rintaro
Production: Toei Doga
129 min

若者は いま 未来へ旅立つ…
The boy leaves for the future...

For Tetsuro Hoshino, eternal life means exchanging his human body for that of a machine, and he sets off to find the very thing. He soon runs into the mysterious Maetel and together they board the Galaxy Express 999 for adventure. The 113-episode TV series lasted two and a half years. ***Galaxy Express 999***, ***Yamato*** and ***Captain Harlock*** are all brainchilds of manga-man Leiji Matsumoto, and so it is befitting that they all take place in the same corner of space. In some episodes, there are character cross-overs and even a bit of nepotism. Maetel, we discover, is in fact the twin sister of Queen Emeraldas, Captain Harlock's antagonist.

Adieu Galaxy Express 999 (1981, Toei)
Sayonara Ginga Tetsudo 999: Andromeda Shuchakueki
Director: Rintaro
Production: Toei Doga
130 min

あれから2年ー青春のロマンをのせて銀河鉄道999はついに最後の旅へ…
Two years have passed - With youthful romance aboard, Galaxy Express departs on its final journey.

Two years have expired since ***Galaxy Express 999*** made its wide-screen debut. In the midst of a raging war between humans and machines, Tetsuro receives a message from Maetel, and again boards the Galaxy Express 999.
Destination: Adventure.

Flyer (7 x 10 inch) $3.00

Flyer (7 x 10 inch) $5.00

Space Battleship Yamato (1977, Toei-Yoga)
Uchuu Senkan Yamato
Director: Toshio Masuda
Production: Office Academy
130 min

地球を救え！はるか宇宙の彼方イスカンダルめざしてヤマトはいま、
ロマンと冒険の旅へ
Save the world! Yamato is headed for the distant planet of Iscandar on a storybook journey of adventure.

The first Yamato feature film, created from the TV series that ran from 1974 to 1975. When radioactive contamination threatens to destroy the planet, the Space Battleship Yamato sets off on a galactic journey to seek a solution. In 2002, Leiji Matsumoto, the originator of Yamato, sued anime producer Yoshinori Nishizaki over the use of his creation. The courts ruled against Matsumoto, claiming it was the content that popularized the many Yamato incarnations.

Farewell to Space Battleship Yamato: In the Name of Love (1978, Toei)
Saraba Uchuu Senkan Yamato: Ai no Senshi Tachi
Director: Toshio Masuda, Tomoharu Katsumata
Production: Office Academy
151 min

永遠の愛とロマンをのせて-ヤマトはいま、
最後の戦いが待つ宇宙のかなたへ…
On a wave of eternal love and adventure, Yamato heads out to its final battle in the far-off universe.

All that stands between The Comet Empire and its planned subjugation of the Universe is Space Battleship Yamato. No surprises to learn that the film, which formed the basis of the second TV series (1978), was not the "farewell" it promised. That didn't prevent four million people crowding the cinemas upon its release.

Poster (20 x 29 inch) $10.00

Be Forever Yamato (1980, Toei)
Yamato yo Towa ni
Director: Tomoharu Katsumata
Production: Office Academy
145 min

空前のスケールに包まれて
いま、ヤマトが帰ってきた!!
On a scale never before seen, Yamato is back!!

The existence of mankind is again threatened, though this time it's that pesky Black Nebula Empire that's invading. In a two-pronged attack, the World Defense Force and Battleship Yamato must save the planet and deal with the appearance of mystery girl Sasha.

Poster (20 x 29 inch) $20.00

Poster (20 x 29 inch) $20.00

Flyer (7 x 10 inch) $1.00

Final Yamato (1983, Toei)
Uchuu Senkan Yamato Kanketsu Hen
Director: Tomoharu Katsumata
Production: West Cape Corporation
152 min

宇宙にひろがる永遠のロマン！
ファイナル・ヤマトの熱い感動をー
いま、あなたに伝えたい…
The never-ending story in the expanse of space! We bring you the moving and emotive Final Yamato...

Set on the watery planet Aquarius, Space Battleship Yamato has a new enemy with which to grapple. Features the resurrection of First Captain Juzo Okita, whose premature passing in the initial film had fans weeping in the aisles. In fact, the film was revised and ***Final Yamato Re-released*** (175 min), the de facto demise of Yamato, was made the same year.

Flyer (7 x 10 inch) $2.00

Toward the Terra (1980, Toei)
Terra e
Director: Hideo Onchi
Production: Toei Doga
119 min

宇宙の潮騒　悲しいまでに広がる星の海　一粒の真珠……地球よ
帰りつくべき故郷への想いー　"われらはよみがえる　地球の土に"
The murmuring of space, in the desolate ocean of stars, one grain of a pearl... It is Earth I long to return to " We will be reborn from the soil of Earth"

Human being Jomy Shin meets The Mu, a preternaturally powerful new-type human, and realizes that this can't be Earth. Soon, humans are at war with their remarkable brethren.

Queen Millennia (1982, Toei)
Sennen Joou
Director: Masayuki Akehi
Production: Queen Millennia Committee
121 min

今、地球は巨大なミステリーにのみこまれる！
Now, Earth is swallowed up in the biggest mystery of all!

Queen Millennia secretly arrives from Lar Metal, a far-off planet that now rules Earth. Her plan is to occupy Earth and launch an attack on her home planet. Another Leiji Matsumoto creation, in the storyline ***Queen Millennia*** immediately predates ***Space Battleship Yamato***.

Flyer (7 x 10 inch) $1.00

Flyer (7 x 10 inch) $1.00

宇宙が熱い！
Space is hot!

The date is 2160. In the distant Ginga Solar System, Crusher is the name given to the space cowboys that run the trans-galaxy lines, guard space ships, remodel planets and deliver pizza. The director is the very same Yoshikazu Yasuhiko who designed the Gundam characters.

Flyer (7 x 10 inch) $1.00

Lensman (1984, Toho-Towa)
SF Shinseiki Lensman
Director: Kazuyuki Hirokawa, Kawajiri Yoshiaki
Production: Kodansha
107 min

84年夏 SF新世紀　未知なる映像は光速で飛来する
Summer, 1984, New Sci-fi Generation
Images never seen before move at light speed

Based on the book by EE "Doc" Smith, Lensman took four years and 1.2 billion yen ($10 million) to make. At the time, the computer graphics it introduced were revolutionary, though they may seem a little lame today.

Odin: Photon Space Sailor Starlight (1985, Toei)
Odin: Koushi Hansen Sailor Starlight
Director: Takeshi Shirato, Eiichi Yamamoto
Production: West Cape Corporation
139 min

北欧神話の謎とロマン！　時空を超えて、いま…
The wonder and appeal of European myth!
Time has passed, and now...

In 2099, a group of pioneering kids sets off on the high seas of space in a sailboat. Their destination is Planet Odin, 180 light years from Earth. Do they survive the trip? Will they find what they're looking for? Does Odin do a decent cup of coffee?

Flyer (7 x 10 inch) $1.00

Flyer (7 x 10 inch) $1.00

Legend of Galactic Heroes: Overture to a New War (1993, Toho)
Ginga Eiyuu Densetsu: Arata Naru Tatakai no Jokyoku
Director: Keizo Shimizu
Production: Tokuma Shoten, Tokuma Japan, Suntory
90 min

人はなぜ英雄となるのかー
What makes a hero...

Adapted from the popular novel by Yoshiki Tanaka, the film features two of anime's most colorful rivals, Reinhardt von Museal, Admiral of the Galactic Fleet, and his nemesis Yang Wen-Li. A new war has broken out, one in which Yang expects to be left to enjoy victory with his buddy Lappe. However, their plans are foiled when they find Commander von Reinhardt lying in wait.

Memories (1995, Shochiku)
Memories
Director: Katsuhiro Otomo
Production: Bandai Visual, Shochiku, Kodansha
115 min

未知からやってくる3つの夢幻世界
Three wonder worlds from the dark unknown

Stink Bomb, ***Cannon Fodder*** and ***Magnetic Rose*** make up this three-in-one collection by Katsuhiro Otomo.

Flyer (7 x 10 inch) $2.00

Flyer (7 x 10 inch) $2.00

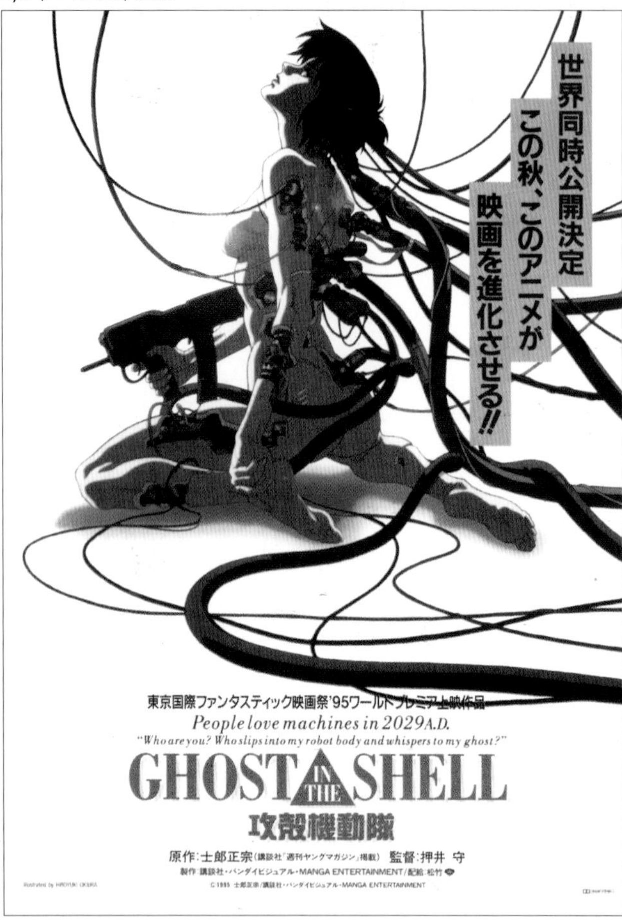

Ghost in the Shell (1995, Shochiku)
Ghost in the Shell: Koukaku Kidou Tai
Director: Mamoru Oshii
Production: Kodansha, Bandai Visual, Manga Entertainment
80 min

世界同時公開決定　この秋、このアニメが映画を進化させる!!
Set for the same-date release throughout the world
This fall, this anime hits the theaters!!

In a world where information networks dominate, cyber terrorism and crime is the norm. Motoko Kusanagi, a cop at Security Police Section 9, goes after the Puppet Master, a mystery hacker whose made it to the top of the world's most-wanted list. GITS was an overwhelming success, reaching the top spot on the US national video selling charts.

Alice (1999, Gaga Communications)
Alice
Director: Kenichi Maejima
Production: Gaga Communications
85 min

コノ未来、私ノセイ？
Is the future my fault?

Alice is the youngest person ever to travel in space. And, when her shuttle crashes, the youngest survivor. She finally makes her way back home after 30 years, but finds a world controlled by computers. So what else is new?

Flyer (7 x 10 inch) $1.00

Flyer (7 x 10 inch) $1.00

愛さずにはいられない。
Can't go on without love.

Robots live alongside humans in Metropolis, a huge city of the future. But it's not all camraderie. Tima, a man-built human, is unaware that the future of Metropolis depends on her.

Metropolis (2001, Toho)
Metropolis
Director: Rintaro
Production: Metropolis Committee
107 min

Flyer (7 x 10 inch) $2.00

Guilstein (2002, Gaga Communications)
Guilstein
Director: Tsuneo Tominaga
Production: Guilstein Committee
90 min

人の心を持った怪物ー　何のために、誰のために、闘うのかー
A monster with a human heart - For what and for whom to fight...

The world of 2088 is a dangerous place. Inhabited by living weapons, known as Guilstein (a fusion of "guilty" and "Frankenstein"), daily life appears to be one long massacre. Chaos, the first Guilstein, is the unlikely named hero. The characters were designed by famed figure creator Yasushi Nirasawa.

Toy Story

Figures, cells, doujinshi: Gotta have 'em all!

Anime just wouldn't be anime without the mega-tons of related goods the medium has spawned. Today, with more than enough on the market to feed a landfill the size of Belgium, these spin-off products can be found almost everywhere, from fast-food outlets to on-line stores. Indeed, the varieties available and their level of sales have become weathervanes of popularity for the individual films they represent. And anime fans, notorious for their willingness to spend, have made many of these seemingly inexpensive items coveted treasures for which no price tag is too ridiculous.

Figures - Hands off my toys!

Figures are popular in Japan because they present a 3-D facsimile of what is ostensibly a 2-D image. So it is somewhat ironic to find that, in the pedantic world of collectors, a virgin figure sealed in its original box fetches twice the price of one that has been soiled by inquisitive fingers. Such is Japan. Figures are also sought after for certain qualities that pertain to the genre. While superheroes should be as life-like as is possible for a small lump of plastic, heroines are prized for their sexiness, however outlandish their vital statistics are. Robot figures, as any self-respecting nerd will tell you, should be overly detailed and weighed down with an arsenal of weaponry.

Some collectors, unsurprisingly, do like to play with their goodies. And so they will purchase two of the same thing - one to touch and one to cherish. Is it any wonder then that the Japanese complain of never having enough space?

Ruri Hoshino (Nadesico) $2,500
This movable, life-size figure was originally priced at five thousand dollars.

Rei Ayanami (Neon Genesis Evangelion) Christmas edition $15.00
Produced for the game center trade, this item is not available for retail.

Rei (Fist of the North Star) $80.00
The limited edition includes a severed head accessory.

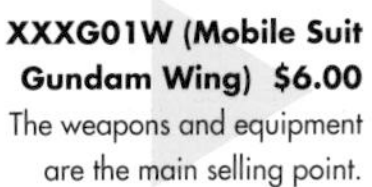

XXXG01W (Mobile Suit Gundam Wing) $6.00
The weapons and equipment are the main selling point.

Cells - The one and only

Cells - pictures drawn onto celluloid sheets and filmed in succession to produce a length of animation - are unique. Literally. Only one of each ever exists. However, the number required to make a feature anime is enormous and the market is now flooded with these images, meaning only a handful can command high prices. Of particular popularity are cells of girl characters that are depicted as directly facing the viewer. Backgrounds are coveted as comparatively few exist (moving characters are superimposed onto a single background that can be used again and again).

One second of animation requires 24 cells. Therefore, for a 30-minute TV anime, accounting for eight minutes of commercials and credits, 31,680 cells are necessary. The process can be shortened by up to 3000 cells by slightly reducing the speed of filming. In the early days of Japanese anime, small budgets forced producers to come up with innovative ideas and technologies which would further reduce costs, while nimble editing could turn an abysmal project into something of reasonable quality. These past efforts to save money have resulted in a situation where, because of their scarcity, cells from particular movies now fetch astronomical prices.

Doujinshi - The real thing, duplicated

Doujinshi is the ultimate otaku medium for self-expression and respectful doffs of the cap to the originators of popular manga. Doujinshi are basically amateur reproductions of favorite manga with new plots and sub-characters added at the whims of their authors. And, as there are few strictures that limit the doujin to a particular storyline or audience, many of these reproductions follow erotic adventures that have catapulted them into the mainstream. Yaoi, for example, which portray male homosexual relations, are extremely popular with inquisitive teenage girls. TV anime would never allow their characters to get up to what they do in the pages of doujinshi. All the better for the doujin, who finds an ever increasing market for her revealing storyboards.

Doujinshi typically sell for $5 to $8 per title. Aficionados, however, will pay over $500 for doujinshi of their choice.

***Mobile Suit Gundam* gets all naughty in this erotic version, Gundam H $7.00**

Forecasting the future, it's safe to say that Studio Ghibli related products will increase in value as will goods that portray the manga characters of 1980s' Shonen Jump issues, the popular weekly magazine. Japan's leading anime goods chain, Mandarake (www.mandarake.co.jp), offers a plethora of anime related goods, and even holds an on-line auction twice-yearly (spring and fall) of rare items. If you can't make it to Japan, then visit their store on the Web.

Fantasy Trip

Amazing, but true

Fantasy anime is escapism on a grand scale. How else could we account for Doraemon, a robot cat with no ears, or Pokemon, eccentric monsters that belong in a child's imagination. Fantastic creatures and mythical characters are the denizens of this fantasy world. Their lives are fairy tales, where the impossible is the mundane, dreams are realities, and the party never ends.

Flyer (7 x 10 inch) $1.00

神は一愛しあう恋人たちを空に放ち星にした…
God - turned the lovers to stars and released them into the sky...

Fairies flutter through the woods and God Apollon rides his flaming chariot across the sky. A heart-warming epic of Greek mythology and romance. The first movie title made by Sanrio, so expect a cameo appearance by Hello Kitty.

Phoenix 2772: Love's Cosmo Zone (1980, Toho)
Hi no Tori 2772: Ai no Cosmo Zone
Director: Taku Sugiyama
Production: Tezuka Production
122 min

Poster (20 x 29 inch) $20.00

Poster (20 x 29 inch) $20.00

オルガよ、おまえも<愛>を知っているのかー
So Orga, you know "love" too...

The future is overpopulated. So having babies is banned. However, a chosen few get to be born and raised in laboratories. One of these lucky ones is Godah, who is brought up alongside Orga, who happens to be a robot. The reason for this is simple: Godah is being taught the Way of the Space Hunter. But not everyone is happy. Rock, a pol down at Government Center, has heard about an energy source in space and sends Godah out to get it. Named Phoenix, and code numbered 2772, this energy source offers the gift of eternal life.

Flyer (7 x 10 inch) $1.00

Unico (1981, Sanrio)
Unico
Director: Toshio Hirata
Production: Sanrio Films
90 min

やさしさと思いやりあふれるユニコ!!
そんなユニコとお友達になってください。
Unico, filled with tender thoughts and kindness!!
Please be friends with Unico.

Direction and original story by Osamu Tezuka. Unico has the power to make people happy, and nice to each other. He's also got a small white horn on his head. And, unsurprisingly, people like Unico, which makes the gods green with envy. Something has to be done about this little upstart, they decide, and so send him away on a long and lonely journey. Sanrio, that maker of Hello Kitty-chans, also liked Unico, and has made a mint flogging his goods to unsuspecting kiddies, many of whom believe he actually exists.

Unico: To the Magic Island (1983, Sanrio)
Unico: Mahou no Shima e
Director: Moribi Murano
Production: Sanrio Films
91 min

心はずむ楽しさ、胸ドキドキのスリル！　幸せ運ぶユニコの愛と冒険！
Wonderfully fun, heart-pounding thrills! The love and adventure of Unico, the bringer of happiness!

Swept away on the Western Wind, Unico is deposited in a village he's never visited before. There, a wicked witch has put a spell on the locals, turning them into slavish puppets who will build a castle for her on a magic island. The unique feeling of terror that this anime elicits is achieved by the use of fairy tale-like imagery, and even adults will find it disturbing. Yoshiaki Kawajiri, famed for action anime such as ***Animatrix*** and ***Vampire Hunter D***, oversaw the visuals.

Flyer (7 x 10 inch) $1.00

Harmagedon (1983, Toho-Towa)
Genma Taisen
Director: Rintaro
Production: Haruki Kadokawa Office
135 min

Flyer (7 x 10 inch) $1.00

Poster (20 x 29 inch) $15.00

幻魔侵攻ーハルマゲドン接近！地球最後の闘いに目覚めよサイオニクス戦士たち！
Demon invasion - Armageddon is nigh! Arise, the psyonics warriors, for the final war of the planet!

Corrupter of the Universe, Genma, meets the psyonicsers in a slugfest. Genma has already wiped out Vega's planet, although he's managed to escape, and now joins forces with the multinational psyonics warriors. Yet another battle to save the Earth. Characters designed by Katsuhiro Otomo, story from the novel by Kazumasa Hirai, manga by Shotaru Ishinomori of ***Cyborg 009*** fame.

Flyer (7 x 10 inch) $1.00

The Country-Star of Cotton (1984, Nihon Herald)
Wata no Kunihoshi
Director: Shinichi Tsuji
Production: Mushi Production
92 min

この子ネコの子、コネコちび猫。猫は人間になれないの？
This girl, a kitten, a small little kitten. Can't cats become human?

Even before she was born, Chibineko believed that there were two types of humans: Those that were born human, and those that had changed from being cats. She is taken in by Tokio Suwano, and out of appreciation decides to make him her lover. But first she must become human... Music by Richard Clayderman, of all people.

Arion (1986, Toho)
Arion
Director: Yoshikazu Yasuhiko
Production: Tokuma Shoten, Hakuhodo, Marubeni, Nippon Sunrise
118 min

昔…神と人とが分たれる以前ー少年がひとり生（いのち）に燃えた!!
Long ago... before humans and gods went their separate ways... a boy burned brightly!!

Based on Greek mythology, the story takes place in the Aegean region of Thrachia and tells of a time long ago when humans and gods lived alongside each other. During yet another war between the gods, a young boy named Arion emerges. On the reverse side of the flyer for ***Arion*** it is claimed that the film will reach even greater heights than ***Nausicaa of the Valley of the Wind***. This, however, turned out to be a bit of wishful PR BS.

Flyer (7 x 10 inch) $1.00

Coo (1993, Toei))
Coo: Tooi Umi kara kita Coo
Director: Tetsuo Imasawa
Production: Kadokawa Shoten, Nihon TV, Bandai Visual, Victor Music Entertainment
116 min

Flyer (7 x 10 inch) $1.00

いつまでも、ずっとそばにいて欲しい…
I want you by my side forever...

Yosuke Obata, who lives with his oceanographer father on the Fijian island of Pago Pago, discovers a strange creature washed up on the beach after a storm. It turns out to be a newly-born Plesiosaurus, a dinosaur thought to have been extinct for some 65 million years. Although the story is based on an adventure novel, it also takes swipes at the nuclear bomb testing that was taking place in the region at the time.

Jungle Emperor Leo (1997, Shochiku)
Jungle Taitei
Director: Yoshio Takeuchi
Production: Tezuka Production
99 min

Flyer (7 x 10 inch) $1.00

This was the first color anime to appear on Japanese TV (the first anime was ***Astro Boy***). The screen version is from the third manga series of the three-generation story of lions ruling over their jungle kingdom. Long ago, Leo's father was murdered by nasty humans. However, at the end of this tearjerker, it is to save one of us that Leo makes the ultimate sacrifice. The film is a fine example of Tezuka Production's skill at showing non-human themes in a sincere and heartrending manner.

Flyer (7 x 10 inch) $1.00

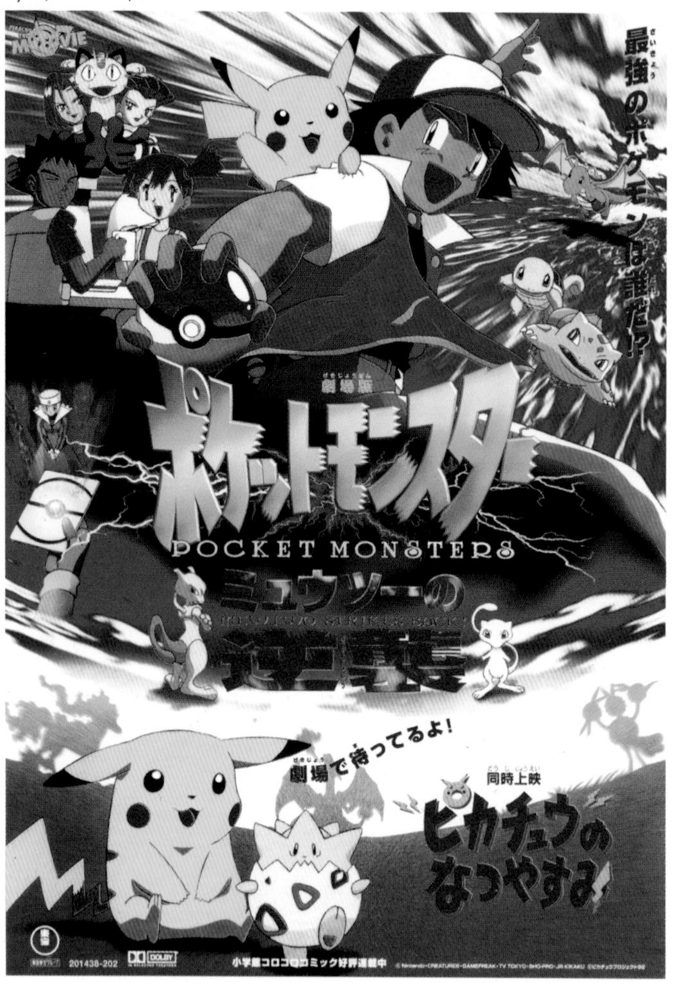

Pokemon: Mewtwo Returns (1998, Toho)
Pocket Monster: Mewtwo no Gyakushuu
Director: Kunihiko Yuyama
Production: Pikachu Project 98
75 min

最強のポケモンは誰だ!?
Who's the strongest Pokemon?!

The anime that launched a thousand tie-ins, this was the first of the Pokemon biggies. The story unfolds with super-strength Mewtwo being created from Mew's fossil. When all's ready, the fighting begins. When Japan Railway launched a Pokemon stamp campaign in cooperation with the film, children swamped stations throughout Tokyo, causing near riots of pre-teen dimensions.

Flyer (7 x 10 inch) $1.00

Pokemon: Revelation Lugia (1999, Toho)
Pocket Monster: Lugia Bakutan
Director: Kunihiko Yuyama
Production: Pikachu Project 1999
81 min

命をかけて、かかってこい!!
Risk your life against me!!

While the three mythological Pokemon birds, Fire, Freezer and Thunder, are kicking the crap out of each other, the oddly shaped Lugia turns up. Is he friend, foe, or simply freak?

Flyer (7 x 10 inch) $1.00

Pokemon: Spell of the Unown
(2000, Toho)
Pocket Monster: Kesshou Tou no Teiou
Director: Kunihiko Yuyama
Production: Pikachu Project 2000
74 min

誰も知らない金と銀の世界をかけろ！
Run through the unknown world of gold and silver!

Mie lives all alone in a huge tower that stands in the resort area, Green Field. Attracted by her, the unidentifiable Pokemon, Unown, arrives and decides to cover the earth in a hard layer of crystal. With box office takings of over 5.8 billion yen, this film proved to be the most popular of the Pokemon series.

Flyer (7 x 10 inch) $1.00

Pokemon: Celebi: A Timeless Encounter (2001, Toho)
Pocket Monster: Celebi: Toki o Koketa Deai
Director: Kunihiko Yuyama
Production: Pikachu Project 2001
99 min

こんなポケモンに逢ってみたかった。
This is the Pokemon we wanted to meet!

Celebi, whose presence leads to the sudden growth of verdant forests brimming with greenery and wildlife, arrives through a timeslip from 40 years past. Team Rockets, of course, try to spoil all the fun. Satoshi and his gang try to prevent them.

Pokemon: Guardian Spirits of the Water Capital: Latias and Latios (2002, Toho)
Pocket Monster: Mizu no Miyako no Mamorigami: Latias to Latios
Director: Kunihiko Yuyama
Production: Pikachu Project 2002
70 min

"心のしずく"が伝説のポケモンを呼びさます。
A tear shed from the heart will bring back the Pokemon myth.

Satoshi and Pikachu run into the siblings Latias and Latios, but are unaware that they secretly guard the Soul Dew that exists only in Altomare, the world's most beautiful (and watery) city.

Poster (20 x 29 inch) $7.00

Alexander (2000, Gaga Comunications)
Alexander Senki
Director: Yoshinori Kanemori, Rintaro
Production: Alexander Committee
102 min

Flyer (7 x 10 inch) $1.00

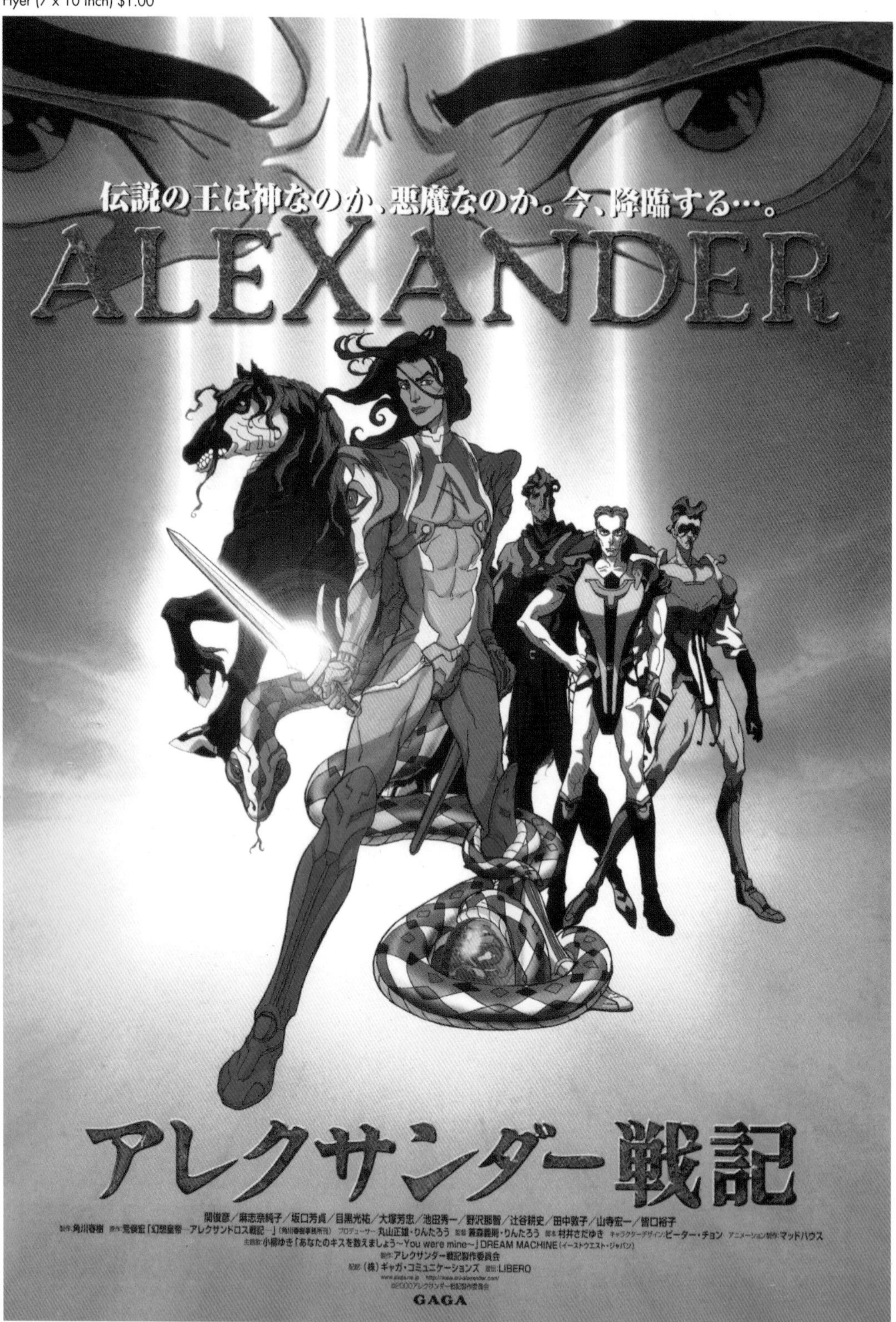

伝説の王は神なのか、悪魔なのか。今、降臨する…。
Is the legendary king a god, or is he a devil? Now, he descends to Earth...

A new and bold interpretation of Alexander the Great and the vast empire that he created. This feature film version brought together creators from Japan, Korea and America on what was a hugely popular production.

Flyer (7 x 10 inch) $1.00

The Boy Who Saw the Wind (2000, Buena Vista International Japan)
Kaze wo Mita Shounen
Director: Kazuki Omori
Production: Hitachi Maxell, Premier International
97 min

ぼくは、いつでも君のそばにいるよ…
I'll always be with you...

Amon has managed to harness an unknown energy source, which makes him a very clever boy indeed. However, the evil dictator, Brannik, has got wind of this awesome power, and hopes to use it to beef up his military might. Amon's not having any of that, and in the end lets rip to destroy Brannik and save what he cherishes.

Tottoko Hamutaro: Hamuhamu Land Adventure (2001, Toho)
Tottoko Hamutaro: Hamuhamu Land Daibouken
Director: Osamu Dezaki
Production: Tottoko 8686 Project 2001
52 min

世界最小のだいぼうけん。
The world's smallest adventure.

Hamutaro is a hamster with a difference: He can understand how humans feel. Which is infuriating because he can't speak their lingo. He desperately wants his owner, Roko, to treat him with more respect. And so he sets off on an adventure to Hamuhamu Land, where he has heard there are sunflower seeds that, when eaten, allow hamsters to communicate with people. After ***Pokemon***, the hamster hordes of Hamuhamu Land are the most-loved anime characters by those old enough to walk. Pop group Minimoni got the break of a lifetime with the release of the catchy theme song.

Flyer (7 x 10 inch) $1.00

Flyer (7 x 10 inch) $1.00

Digimon Adventure 02 (2000, Toei)
Digimon Adventure 02
Director: Yamauchi Shigeyasu
Production: 2000 Summer Toei Anime Fair Committee
65 min

驚異の新デジモン誕生！
A threatening new Digimon comes to life!

Digimon is the animated version of the computer game in which players create and train digital monsters for battle. The anime story is broken into two parts and follows the adventures of these virtual monsters as they tear up America. Although initially viewed as a rehash of ***Pokemon***, Digimon quickly established its own international fan base.

Tree of Palme (2002, Toho)
Palme no Ki
Director: Takashi Nakamura
Production: Tree of Palme Committee
136 min

人間に、なりたい。
I want to become human.

Like Pinocchio, Palme is a doll with human aspirations. Created by a botanist for his sick wife, Palme isn't much satisfied with his lot and departs to the netherworld, known as Tamas. Written and directed by Takashi Nakamura, the man behind ***Harmagedon*** and ***Akira***.

Flyer (7 x 10 inch) $1.00

Flyer (7 x 10 inch) $1.00

Doraemon: Nobita and the Robot Kingdom (2002, Toho)
Doraemon: Nobita to Robot Kingdom
Director: Tsutomu Shibayama
Production: Shinei Doga, Shogakukan, TV Asahi
80 min

そこは、すごいロボットだらけの国。
It's a country full of amazing robots.

The queen hates robots. Which is a pity, because they live happily alongside humans in this fantasy domain. But when she decrees that all robots must be shorn of their emotions, boy-robot Poko flees in fear. He crosses time and space and ends up, lost and confused, in the world of Doraemon and his gang. This is the 23rd installment in the long-running series, and is reflected in the age of its narrators, all of whom are over 60 years old.

Doraemon: Nobita and the Magical Windmaster (2003,Toho)
Doraemon: Nobita to Fushigi Kazetsukai
Director: Tsutomu Shibayama
Production: Shinei Doga, Shogakukan, TV Asahi
80 min

風のドラえもん、はじまる。
Doraemon on the wind, begins.

Nobita meets the Typhoon Girl, and nicknames her Fu-ko. Together with Doraemon, he takes her through the Dokodemo Door and across an endless plain until they finally reach a strange village. Here, the inhabitants have the power to control the wind. And it is also here that a war breaks out between the good People of the Wind and the evil Storm Tribe. Suneo seems his same old self, but then something happens...

Flyer (7 x 10 inch) $1.00

Tall Dark Strangers

The good, the bad, and the animated

Anime is peppered with tough guys, those who favor action over words, who shoot first and don't bother with questions. Vampire Hunter D and Golgo 13 are loners of few words and dark demeanors. Kenshin Himuro and Joe Yabuki are men of conviction, who fight for what they believe is right. Some pass through life in silence - unsmiling outsiders who rarely seek glory from their heroic actions. Others are bounty hunters - in it for the money and to hell with justice. But all are proof, if need be, that anime is not a medium for kids alone.

Captain Harlock: Mystery of the Arcadia (1978, Toei)
Captain Harlock: Arcadia Go no Nazo
Director: Tomonori Imada
Production: Toei Doga
34 min

Poster (20 x 29 inch) $20.00

男なら、生命をかけて戦わなければならない時がある…
When you're a man, you've sometimes got to stand up and fight...

The adventures of space pirate Captain Harlock and his band of cut-throats. Astute viewers may find some scenes similar to the 13-part TV series, ***The Evil Castle on the Sea of Death***. The original is by ***Galaxy Express 999*** creator, Leiji Matsumoto.

Tomorrow's Joe (1980, Nihon Herald, Fuji Eiga)
Ashita no Joe
Director: Youichiro Fukuda
Production: Herald Enterprise, Sankyo Eiga, Fuji Eiga
153 min

Flyer (7 x 10 inch) $1.00

Flyer (7 x 10 inch) $1.00

まっかに燃えあがれ！ジョー！
Burn red hot! Joe!

The story follows the development of rookie boxer Joe Yabuki, and the characters he meets in and out of the ring. Reworked for the big screen, the action builds to the final bout that sees Joe pitted against his arch rival, Rikiishi. The original comic book series was so popular that when Rikiishi was killed off an actual funeral was held.

Flyer (7 x 10 inch) $1.00

Tomorrow's Joe 2 (1981, Nihon Herald)
Ashita no Joe 2
Director: Osamu Dezaki
Production: Herald Enterprise, Sankyo Eiga, Fuji Eiga, Chiba Planning
110 min

いま、君は帰って行くーまだ見たことのない母のもとへ…
勇気をありがとう　ジョー。
As you leave to meet your maker... Thanks for your courage, Joe.

Rikiishi's death marks the end of the first series. Joe then goes on to fight some of his toughest opponents - Carlos Rivera, Kin Ryuhi, Harimao and Jose Mendoza. In a plot that is fast-paced to the end, Joe leaves no score unsettled.

Flyer (7 x 10 inch) $1.00

Arcadia of My Youth (1982, Toei)
Waga Seishun no Arcadia
Director: Tomoharu Katsumata
Production: Toei, Tokyu Agency
130 min

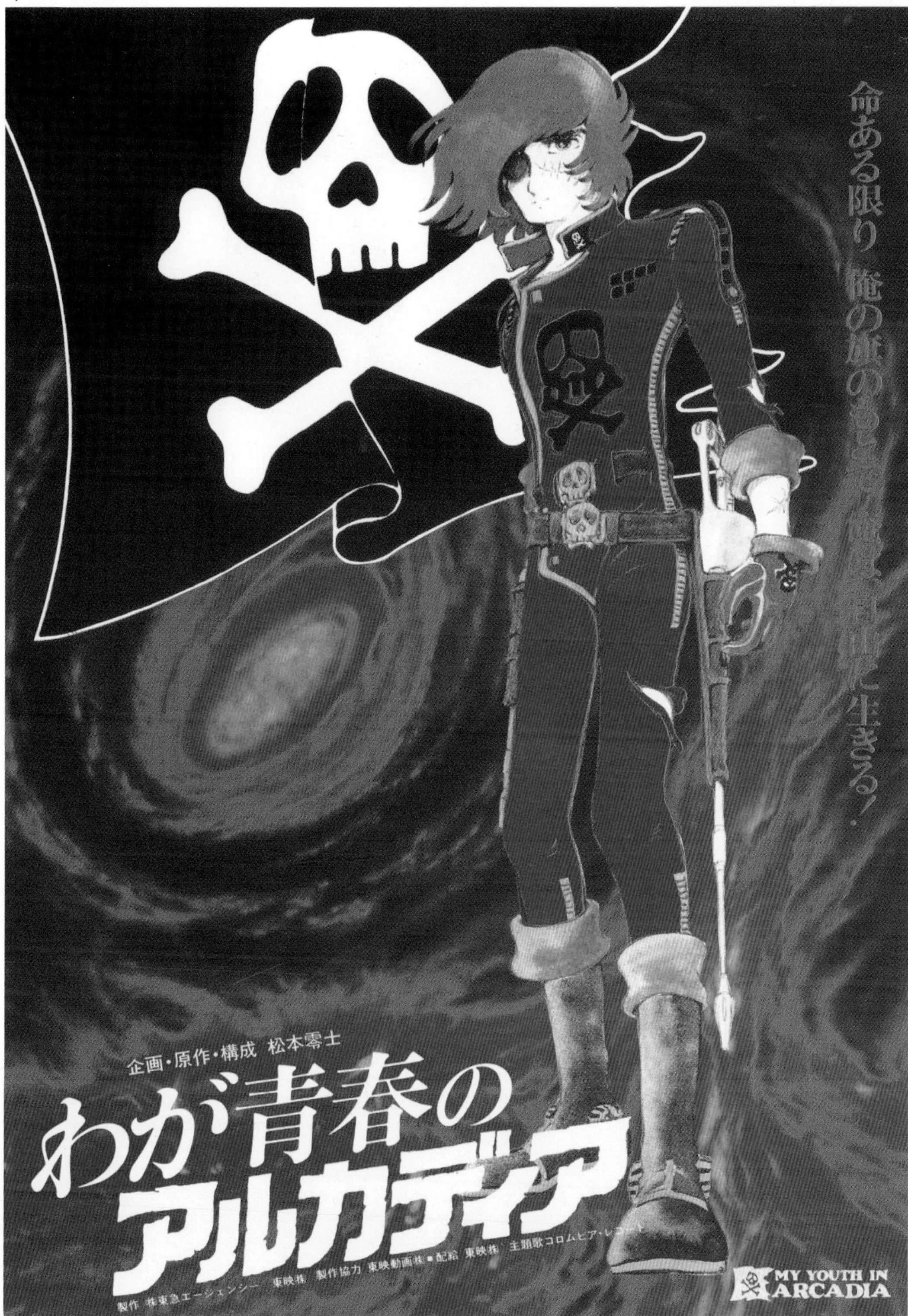

命ある限り　俺の旗のもとで　俺は、自由に生きる！
I will live in freedom, under my own flag, for the rest of my life.

Following his 1978 TV series and guest appearance on ***Galaxy Express 999***, Captain Harlock was ready to storm the movie theaters. In this second feature, Harlock`s adventures lead to friendship and love, for which the loss of an eye is a small price to pay. The Captain has proved to be Leiji Matsumoto`s most enduring character, and although this film is said to depict his early years he still comes across as a grizzled, tough guy with an eye for the ladies (no pun intended). Fans hoping to see him at his most swashbuckling, however, may feel slightly cheated.

Flyer (7 x 10 inch) $1.00

Space Adventure Cobra (1982, Toho-Towa)
Space Adventure Cobra
Director: Osamu Dezaki
Production: Tokyo Movie Shinsha
103 min

激射<サイコガン>!大銀河系を無敵のニューヒーローが走る!
Blasting Psycho Gun! The invincible new hero speeds through the galaxy!

Space pirate Cobra's left arm is in fact a Psycho Gun, a meaty weapon that he uses to defend himself and his buddies, Armroid and Lady, as they traverse the galaxy in their trusty Turtle spaceship. And if that's not enough, it all takes place in Dolby Sound, the first for an anime.

Golgo 13 (1983, Toho-Towa)
Golgo 13
Director: Osamu Dezaki
Production: Tokyo Movie Shinsha, Film Link
95 min

世界を揺がす!ー超A級の興奮が襲いかかる!
Shake up the world! Triple A excitement takes you over!

Nothing is known of Golgo 13 except his profession - sniper. The FBI, CIA and Pentagon are pissed, and set out to hunt him down before he can carry out another killing.

Flyer (7 x 10 inch) $1.00

Flyer (7 x 10 inch) $1.00

Dagger of Kamui (1985, Toei)
Kamui no Ken
Director: Rintaro
Production: Haruki Kadokawa Office
132 min

Poster (20 x 29 inch) $15.00

Poster (20 x 29 inch) $15.00

めざめよー冒険心。
Awake - Adventurous Spirit.

Produced on a grand scale, this adventure story moves from the rolling hills of Japan to the arctic wastelands of Alaska. All alone in the world, ninja Jiro goes in search of the treasure of Captain Kidd, but must battle a torrent of enemies if he is to reach his goal.

Black Jack (1996, Shochiku)
Black Jack
Director: Osamu Dezaki
Production: Tezuka Production, Shochiku
93 min

Flyer (7 x 10 inch) $1.00

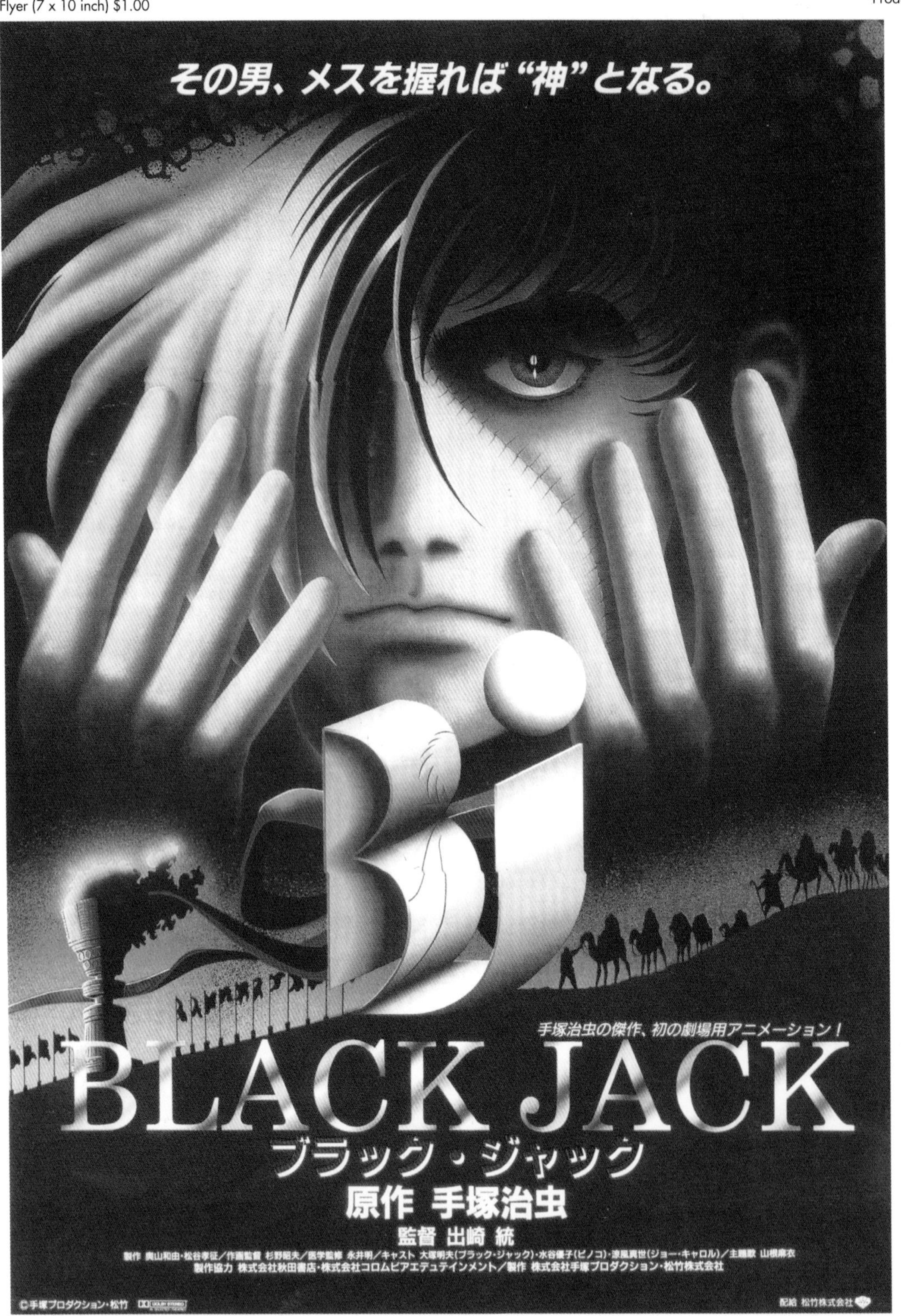

その男、メスを握れば"神"となる。
With scalpel in hand, he becomes a "god".

Although unlicensed, Black Jack has a god-given gift for surgery. When super humans, who have exceeded in their fields, be it sports, science or art, because of a certain chemical that exists in their brains, break down, Black Jack takes out his trusty scalpel. Compulsory viewing for med students.

Flyer (7 x 10 inch) $1.00

Perfect Blue (1997, Rex Entertainment)
Perfect Blue
Director: Satoshi Kon
Production: Rex Entertainment
81 min

もう自分のことがわからない。
I know nothing about myself anymore.

Aspiring actress Mima Kirigoe announces her decision to quit Cham, a pop group with little claim to fame. But her career move is dampened by a string of murders, as those around her get knocked off one by one. And it only gets weirder when she's confronted by her mirror image, dressed in her former costume and going by the name of Mami.

Samurai X: The Warrior's Heart (1997, Sony Pictures Entertainment)
Rurouni Kenshin: Meiji Kenkaku Romantan: Ishin Shishi he no Requiem
Director: Hatsuki Tsuji
Production: Fuji TV, SPE Visual Works
90 min

眠れぬ志士よ、逆刃に問え！
The samurai that never sleeps demands the other side of the blade!

An action samurai flick (a style known as *chanbara*) based on the story of wandering samurai legend Kenshin Himuro. Visiting Yokohama with his sword-wielding gang, Kenshin runs into the sister of a former victim. Blood and guts guaranteed.

Flyer (7 x 10 inch) $1.00

Jin-Roh (1999, Bandai Visual, Media Box)
Jin-Roh
Director: Hiroyuki Okiura
Production: Bandai Visual, ING
98 min

Flyer (7 x 10 inch) $1.00

獣としての宿命を背負った男と　愛を夢みた女の物語ー。
The story of an animal of a man and a woman with a dream of love...

Anti-terrorist Unit Special Agent Kazuki Fuse has always followed his killer instincts and obeyed orders. But all this changes in an encounter he has when on the hunt for a criminal gang. Suddenly he starts to see his life in a very different light. Original story and script by Mamoru Oshii.

Blood: The Last Vampire (2000, Sony Pictures Entertainment)
Blood: The Last Vampire
Director: Hiroyuki Kitakubo
Production: SPE Visual Works, Sony Computer Entertainment, IG Plus, Information-Technology Promotion Agency Japan
48 min

Flyer (7 x 10 inch) $1.00

斬るーそれが少女の宿命
To kill - that is the girl's fate.

It's 1966, and the war rages in Vietnam. At the Yokota American Air Base in Japan, a number of unexplained suicides have taken place. A secret society that fights vampires believes there's more to the deaths than meets the eye, and Saya, a young girl with a lot of balls, is dispatched to the American School to investigate. There she finally comes face to face with her prey, and wields her sword like only a young girl can...

Vampire Hunter D: Bloodlust (2001, Nihon Herald)
Vampire Hunter D
Director: Yoshiaki Kawajiri
Production: Vampire Hunter D Committee
103 min

Flyer (7 x 10 inch) $1.00

暗黒の闇を切り裂く孤独の狩人。
The lone hunter rips through the night's darkness.

Adapted from part III of Hideyuki Kikuchi's series of novels, Vampire Hunter. A young half-vampire, who goes by the name of Vampire Hunter D, dedicates his weekends to ridding the world of bloodsucking creeps.

Cowboy Bebop: Knockin' on Heaven's Door (2001, Sony Pictures Entertainment)
Cowboy Bebop: Tengoku no Tobira
Director: Shinichiro Watanabe
Production: Sunrise, Bones, Bandai Visual
114 min

Flyer (7 x 10 inch) $1.00

Flyer (7 x 10 inch) $1.00

それは、聖者のような悪魔だった
It was a saint-like devil

Mars, 2071. The government has put out a reward of 300 million woolong for the capture of a terror group and its leader that have developed biological weapons. Spike Spiegel and his motley crew of bounty hunters, Jet Black, Faye Valentine, Ed and Ein, get wind of the reward and throw their spaceship, Bebop, into top gear.

Retro-Specs

Look back in wonder

The Japanese have a saying, "Study the old to learn the new" (*on ko chi shin*). The technology and know-how that each year produces more astounding anime owes everything to the films of the past. Watched even today, classic titles such as One Thousand and One Arabian Nights, Battle of the Planets and Future Boy Conan, which debuted in the '60s and '70s, remain remarkably vivid and poignant. Needless to say, they will continue giving pleasure for generations to come.

Poster (20 x 29 inch) $80.00

ひと飛び空を三千里！　ぼくは悟空だ強いんだ　ふしぎな術でわるものたちをやっつける！
A million mile glide! I'm the powerful Goku, who punishes evil with my magical chant!

Based on the well-known Chinese story of Son Goku, the monkey, and Sanzo Hoshi, the monk, who travel to Tenjiku (today's India) to receive a blessed sutra. The story centers on the development of Goku's personality and mind. And how he uses his newfound inner strengths to kick ass like only a wise monkey can. Osamu Tezuka contributed much to the success of the film, and was on hand at the Vienna Children's Film Festival for the Special Grand Prize.

Poster (20 x 29 inch) $60.00

Tobimaru and the Fox with Nine Tails (1968, Daiei)
Kyuubi no Kitsune to Tobimaru
Director: Gentaro Nakajima
Production: Nihon Doga
81 min

嵐を呼び火を吹いて暴れ狂う巨像の正体は？美しい少女の魔力の謎は？
驚異の大スペクタクルで描く話題のアクション動画！
Who is the giant calling up a storm, breathing fire and running wild? What is the secret of the beautiful girl's magic power? The greatest action movie of its time!

Set in the Heian era, the Devil is using the young beauty Tamamo and a Buddhist image in an attempt to take over the world. But Tobimaru, Tamamo's childhood sweetheart, has other ideas.

One Thousand and One Arabian Nights (1969, Nihon Herald)
Sen-ya Ichi-ya Monogatari
Director: Eiichi Yamamoto
Production: Mushi Production
130 min

映画史上初めての手法<アニメラマ>で描く
美とエロチシズム溢れる陶酔の2時間！
For the first time in world cinematography comes a two-hour animerama of beauty and eroticism.

Japan's most prominent manga artist, Tezuka Osamu, made his feature anime debut on this steamy adults-only picture. It was one of many categorized as "animerama" (anime and drama).

Poster (20 x 29 inch) $50.00

The Little Mermaid, Great Mazinger vs Getter Robo, Ganbare Robocon, etc. (1975, Toei)

Poster (20 x 29 inch) $35.00

The Forest Lives, Galaxy Express 999: Claire of Glass, Masked Rider, etc. (1996, Toho)

Poster (20 x 29 inch) $20.00

Ali Baba and the 40 Thieves, Grendizer Getter Robo Great Mazinger: Decisive Battle of the Great Monster of the Sea, Secret Task Force Goranger, etc. (1976, Toei)

Poster (20 x 29 inch) $22.00

Prince of Swan, The Ultimate Combattler-V, Dokaben, etc (1977, Toei)

Poster (20 x 29 inch) $22.00

The Humpbacked Horse, Planet Robot Danguard Ace vs Insect Robot Army, Candy Candy, etc. (1977, Toei)

Poster (20 x 29 inch) $15.00

Thumbelina, Planet Robot Danguard Ace: Great Naval Space Battle, Ikkyu-san and Naughty Princess, etc. (1978, Toei)

Poster (20 x 29 inch) $15.00

A festival of anime brought to the silver screen by the trailblazers of Japanese anime, Toei Studios. The festivals would appear each spring and summer holiday, and would be an assemblage of TV anime digests, fairy tales from around the world and special effects hero anime shown reel to reel. The festivals began in 1967 to celebrate the 10th anniversary of Toei's founding. March, 1990 saw the last Anime Matsuri, as that summer the carnival was renamed Anime Fair, and has continued so ever since.

Little Remi and Capi the Dog (1970, Toei)
Chibikko Remi to Meiken Capi
Director: Hiroshi Okawa
Production: Toei Doga
81 min

Poster (20 x 29 inch) $25.00

花がさくころ！レミとカピのたのしい冒険まんがが見られます
The season of flowers! Remi and Kapi's fun adventure manga

An adaptation of Hector Malot's ***Remi the Homeless Girl*** from the torch bearers of early Japanese anime, Toei Studios. The story follows the friendship of Remi and her dog Kapi. The poster's shape is rare even today.

Poster (20 x 29 inch) $40.00

Devil Dog Liner 0011 (1972, Toei)
Maken Liner 0011 Henshin Seyo!
Director: Hiroshi Okawa
Production: Toei Doga
50 min

ぼくはツトム……超スーパー犬四匹といっしょに斗うぞ！敵は！地球侵略を狙うゴルゴス星人だ
I'm Tsutomu...... Fighting with my 4 super dogs! The enemy! Alien Gorgoths seeking to take over Earth!

When Tsutomu's father, Dr. Hayashi, is attacked by aliens, his brave dog Queen sacrifices herself and her three puppies to save him. Out of gratitude, the doctor revives the dogs and turns them into powerful cyborg canines. When they take on the wicked and despotic, the dogs merge to form the jet fighter "Cyborg Dog Liner". And so it is against the Devil Aliens, who threaten Earth with invasion and bad hair. Theme music composer Takeo Yamashita was behind the score of the first ***Lupin III*** TV series.

Flyer (7 x 10 inch) $4.00

Belladonna of Sadness (1973, Nihon Herald)
Kanashimi no Belladonna
Director: Eiichi Yamamoto
Production: Mushi Production, Nihon Herald
89 min

悪魔に身体を捧げ、異様な快楽の中で愛に泣くジャンヌ！
新鮮な題材を、世界に類をみない大胆な手法で描く
アニメ・スペクタクル！
Sacrificing her flesh to the Devil, Jeane weeps for love as she indulges her peculiar pleasures. With fresh subject matter, it is an anime spectacle made with techniques used for the first time in the world.

One of the "animerama" series created with adults in mind. The last film produced by Mushi Production before it went under, the film portrays the picture book art of illustrator Kuni Fukai, albeit in animation.

Bell of Chirin (1978, Nihon Herald)
Chirin no Suzu
Director: Masami Hata
Production: Sanrio Films
46 min

弱い羊なんていやだ！　ぼくは強くなりたいんだ
狼のウォーと戦っても、ぜったい負けない羊に！
I hate being a weak sheep!
I`m gonna become strong and fight against the wolves.
I will win!

Chirin is a lamb with attitude. When a wolf kills his mother, he goes in search of sweet revenge. Gives a new meaning to "lamb chop." The writer, Takashi Yanase, is better known as the creator of ***Anpanman***.

Poster (20 x 29 inch) $15.00

Flyer (7 x 10 inch) $3.00

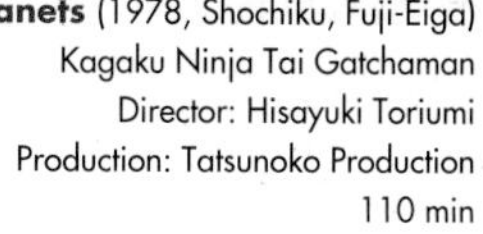

Battle of the Planets (1978, Shochiku, Fuji-Eiga)
Kagaku Ninja Tai Gatchaman
Director: Hisayuki Toriumi
Production: Tatsunoko Production
110 min

翔べ！火の鳥　紅の炎　遥かなるロマンの大宇宙へー
Fly! Phoenix, red flame, to the never-ending story of outer space

President X has an extraordinary plan by which to conquer Earth. He wants to blow it up, thus causing the creation of a black hole. What he hasn't planned for is Gatchaman, a group of five ninja scientists who aren't too keen on dying and decide to do something to stop him. The anime had long-lasting appeal, and Gatchaman has appeared more recently in Tatsunoko Production's ***Tatsunoko Babies***.

Flyer (7 x 10 inch) $5.00

Future Boy Conan (1979, Toei)
Mirai Shounen Conan
Director: Hajime Sato
Production: Nihon Animation
123 min

走れ！飛べ！戦え！コナン　平和と自然がよみがえるまでー君には
愛するラナや素敵な仲間　そして、ぼくらも一緒についている！
Run! Fly! Fight! Conan Until peace and nature is restored - You have your loving Lana and your friends, and we'll always be with you too!

Based on ***The Incredible Tide*** by Alexander Key, Conan roams through nature free as a cloud. When he meets Lana, his life becomes one of love and adventure. The TV series ended after 26 episodes, inciting 100,000 letters from soppy but irate viewers. Hayao Miyazaki was involved with character design and screen effects.

Triton of the Sea (1979, West Cape Corporation)
Umi no Triton
Director: Yoshinobu Nishizaki
Production: West Cape Corporation
74 min

限りない謎とロマンを秘めて
愛と平和のために闘う少年トリトンの夢と冒険の旅！
Searching for a never-ending story of mystery
Triton's dream adventure, fighting for love and peace!

Leagues beneath the ocean, the two mermen tribes, the Tritons and the Poseidons, wage war and smash-mouth. A grand anime with an abundance of celebs: Produced and directed by Yoshinobu Nishizaki of the Yamato series, supervised by Toshio Masuda (also of Yamato fame) and Toshio Masuda (Gundam), and written by Osamu Tezuka.

Poster (20 x 29 inch) $20.00

Animation Nation

Who's Who in Anime

Since its emergence less than 50 years ago, Japanese anime has gained worldwide fame. But as with any venture, success didn't come without the behind-the-scenes rivalry, respect, support, and friendships that run deep.

"Spirited Away -- Miyazaki's last great effort"

This was the opinion at least of Hayao Miyazaki's close friend, Mamoru Oshii, after the film made box-office history. In light of their friendship, which goes back to the days before Miyazaki started out on his own, the comment is not without a hint of praise. And Oshii himself is no envious critic waiting in the wings for his friend's demise. His work on ***Blood: The Last Vampire*** was overly praised by Katsuhiro Otomo, and placed him up there with the big guns of Japanese animation.

The world of anime is close-knit, and in many ways self-propagating. Hideaki Anno's ***Neon Genesis Evangelion*** was greatly inspired by Yoshiyuki Tomino's Ideon. In the film one can also see the influences of ***Nausicaa: Valley of the Wind***, in the creation of which Anno played a lead role. Miyazaki, on the other hand, claimed it was ***Nausicaa*** that owed much to the vision of Osamu Tazuka. Both, it turns out, were Japanese anime trailblazers, and both cut their teeth at Toei Doga.

Tezuka, who, undeniably, launched televised anime, went on to found Mushi Productions. It was there that Osamu Dezaki, ***Ideon***'s Tomino and numerous other talented animators found their niche and an environment in which to develop. Placed in charge of screen play on ***Triton of the Sea***, Tomino discovered an element in which his talents could mature, and in doing so he joined the growing list of anime greats.

But not all was storybook success and fame. Producer of ***Triton***, Yoshinobu Nishizaki, allowed fantasy to get the better of him. When he was arrested for possession of firearms and stimulants, he claimed in his defense that he had a duty to rid the planet of "pirates." Leiji Matsumoto, the originator of ***Mobile Suit Gundam***, also ended up in court with Nishizaki over the rights to his work.

Matsumoto lost his appeal but went on to make ***Galaxy Express 999***, directed by Rintaro, a buddy of Tezuka from the Toei Doga days. Rintaro was behind ***Metropolis*** and ***Harmagedon***, in both of which Katsuhiro Otomo had a hand. Otomo's passions are not limited to anime. A keen cyclist, when he's not weaving together another hit movie, he can be seen peddling alongside his bicycling buddy Miyazaki in the suburbs of Tokyo.

Hayao Miyazaki is known for the opportunities he offers young directors, who, he hopes, will learn the business through experience and hard work. In this way, what Miyazaki and his fellow animators have brought to life will continue to develop and inspire in the many years to come.

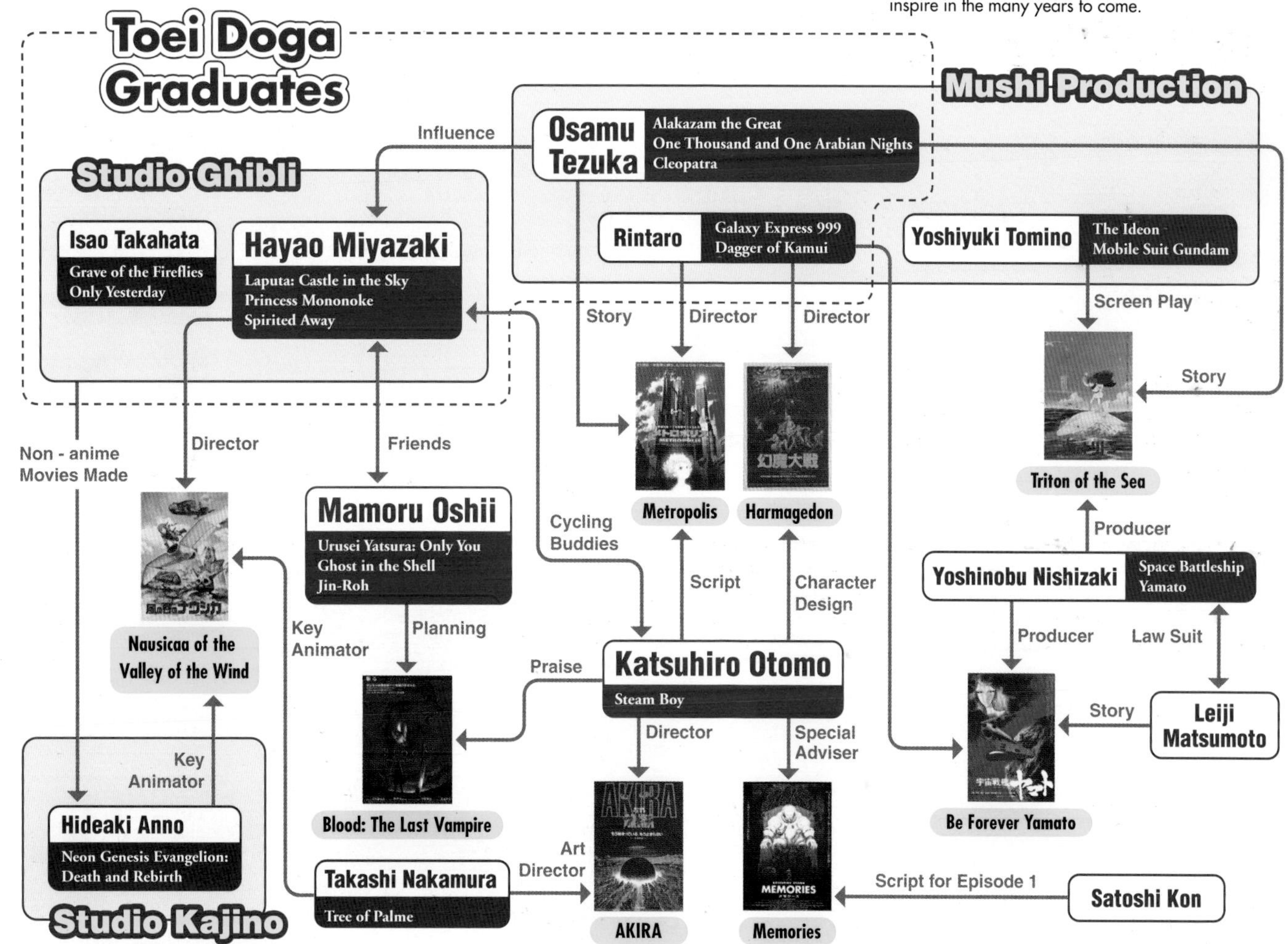

And I'd like to thank...

Studio Ghibli was founded in 1985 by world-renowned anime artists Hayao Miyazaki and Isao Takahata. The word itself (pronounced "jibli") has its roots in the Sahara, where it describes the hot wind that sweeps across the desert. It is an apt choice. For almost two decades, Studio Ghibli has breathed fresh ideas into the anime world with such greats as Nausicaa, Spirited Away and Princess Mononoke.

Nausicaa of the Valley of the Wind (1984, Toei)
Kaze no Tani no Nausicaa
Director: Hayao Miyazaki
Production: Top Craft
116 min

Poster (20 x 29 inch) $15.00

Poster (20 x 29 inch) $15.00

少女の愛が奇跡を生んだ…
The girl's love brought about a miracle...

After mechanized civilization has been destroyed, and the world is covered with contaminated oceans, the time is right for evil to fulfill its destiny to rule the planet. But not if Nausicaa, a young woman with big ideas, can put a stop to it. Battle ensues, as it always does at these moments. The scene where resurrected god-warrior Kyoshinhei destroys Ohmu was created by Hideaki Anno of ***Evangelion*** fame. The success of the film launched Studio Ghibli's career.

Program (8 x 11 inch) $12.00

Flyer (7 x 10 inch) $4.00

Laputa: Castle in the Sky (1986, Toei)
Tenkuu no Shiro Laputa
Director: Hayao Miyazaki
Production: Studio Ghibli
124 min

Deep down in the mine where he toils, Pazu meets Sheeta, who has in her possession the Levitation Stone, a mystical rock that both the Government and a band of pirates (the two are not to be confused) are after. The film follows the adventures of the two kids as they do everything they can to hang on to the stone and eventually reach the mythical floating island of Laputa. Pazu is narrated by none other than Mayumi Tanaka, credited for the voice of such characters as ***Dragon Ball***'s Kurillin, Luffy of ***One Piece***, and many other well-known boy characters.

Program (8 x 11 inch) $15.00

Flyer (7 x 10 inch) $4.00

My Neighbor Totoro (1986, Toei)
Tonari no Totoro
Director: Hayao Miyazaki
Production: Studio Ghibli
88 min

Grave of the Fireflies (1988, Toho)
Hotaru no Haka
Director: Isao Takahata
Production: Studio Ghibli
88 min

このへんないきものは、まだ日本にいるのです。たぶん。
This strange creature still lives in Japan...I think.

Together with their father, the two sisters Satsuki and Mei move to the countryside, where nature is still abundant and life moves at an unhurried pace. There, the girls come across a kind-hearted forest-dwelling creature called Totoro, and their lives are never the same. The story is set in May of 1955, a date that influenced the naming of the lead characters Mei ("May" in English) and Satsuki ("The Fifth Month" in Japanese). Visitors to the Studio Ghibli Museum in Mitaka are ferried to the site in a bus designed to resemble the film's Neko Bus.

4歳と14歳で、生きようと思った。
At ages 4 and 14, they decided to live.

14-year-old Seita and his 4-year-old sister, Setsuko, have lost their mother in the aerial bombings of 1945 and must struggle to survive the closing days of the war and its aftermath. Based on the Naoki Award-winning novel by Akiyuki Nosaka, the film is a guaranteed tearjerker that will remain with you long after you leave the theater. Bring a towel.

Flyer (7 x 10 inch) $1.50

Kiki's Delivery Service (1989, Toei)
Majo no Takkyubin
Director: Hayao Miyazaki
Production: Studio Ghibli
103 min

おちこんだりもしたけれど、私はげんきです。
I was despondent, but now I'm doing fine.

Anime maestro Hayao Miyazaki's film is based on the children's book of the same name by Eiko Kakuno. The story follows the development of Kiki, a 13-year-old witch who visits the human world on her broomstick and has a cat named Jiji that sold enormous amounts of character goods to addled children.

Only Yesterday (1991, Toho)
Omoide Poroporo
Director: Isao Takahata
Production: Studio Ghibli
119 min

私はワタシと旅にでる。
Myself and I leave on a journey.

27-year-old working girl, Taeko Okajima, is having second thoughts about her life. Fondly recalling her time as a 5th grader back in her hometown, she decides to return for a few days to think about what she really wants. Oh, if only it were that simple...

Flyer (7 x 10 inch) $1.00

Porco Rosso (1992, Toho)
Kurenai no Buta
Director: Hayao Miyazaki
Production: Studio Ghibli
93 min

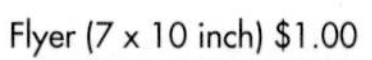
Flyer (7 x 10 inch) $1.00

カッコイイとは、こういうことさ。
This is what we call groovy!

Set in First World War Italy, an ex-air force ace casts a spell on himself that will have peculiar results. He turns into a pig, and Porco Rosso, the flying swine, is born. In the French language version of this story about a pilot who shuns fame and becomes a pig, the lead role is narrated by Jean Reno.

Flyer (7 x 10 inch) $1.00

Pom Poko (1994, Toho)
Heisei Tanuki Gassen Pompoko
Director: Isao Takahata
Production: Studio Ghibli
119 min

タヌキだってがんばってるんだよォ。
Tanuki are trying hard too!

When a housing development project threatens a colony of tanuki (a type of raccoon), the animals revive their ancient shape-changing skills to confront the human invaders. Pom Poko took first prize for feature anime at France's Annecy International Anime Festival in 1995.

Whispers of the Heart (1995, Toho)
Mimi wo Sumaseba
Director: Yoshifumi Kondo
Production: Studio Ghibli
119 min

好きなひとが、できました。
I've found someone to love.

Shizuku loves books. But when she befriends junior high classmate Seiji, whose dream is to be a violinist, she starts to think about her own future. Unlike most Ghibli films, Whispers was based on *shojo* manga, the distinctly girl-oriented comics of Japan. Focusing on the young, and how they face the realities of the future, its audience was overwhelmingly teenage and female.
Lots of "ooos" and "aaaaghs".

Poster (20 x 29 inch) $15.00

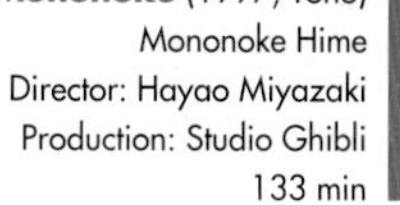

Princess Mononoke (1997, Toho)
Mononoke Hime
Director: Hayao Miyazaki
Production: Studio Ghibli
133 min

Flyer (7 x 10 inch) $1.00

生きろ。
Live.

A deep, dark forest inhabited by gods is threatened by an invasion of warring humans. Among the chaos that unfolds, Sun, a young girl raised by wild beasts, meets her young man, Ashitaka. Miyazaki announced it to be his last film. But in the tradition of anime, where nothing really ever ends, he forges on.

Flyer (7 x 10 inch) $1.00

Spirited Away (2001, Toho)
Sen to Chishiro no Kamikakushi
Director: Hayao Miyazaki
Production: Studio Ghibli
125 min

トンネルのむこうは、不思議の町でした。
Beyond the tunnel was a town of wonder.

Oscar winner for best animated feature film at the 75th Annual Academy Awards (if you didn't know already...), the movie takes place in a strange town where the gods come to bathe and cure their ills. Into this town arrive Chihiro and her parents, who subsequently become pigs. When the DVD was first released in Japan, the color quality was of a slightly redder tinge than the original film, and subsequently became a court case.

The Cat Returns (2002, Toho)
Neko no Ongaeshi
Director: Hiroyuki Morita
Production: Studio Ghibli
125 min

猫の国。それは、自分の時間を生きられないやつの行くところ。
猫になっても、いいんじゃないッ？
The land of cats. It's a place where those who can't live in their own time go. I suppose I could try being a cat too!

An action-free cat-lovers anime again based on *shojo* manga, the film is a sister production of ***Whispers of the Heart***, and even features the Baron. High school student Haru helps a moggie in distress, and in reward is invited to The Land of the Cats. Not for those with fur allergies.

Flyer (7 x 10 inch) $1.00

INDEX 日本語タイトル

INDEX Romanized Titles

INDEX

English Titles

http://www.dhp-online.com

Available from DH Publishing inc.

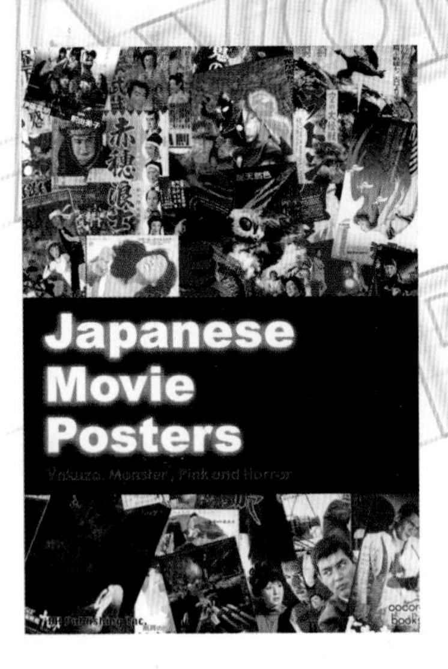

cocoro books

Japanese Movie Posters

Yakuza, Monster, Pink and Horror

A tribute to 50 years of lurid imagery and purple prose created by nameless designers at Japanese film studios. Unforgettable images conjured out of a few still photos, some bold lettering, and plenty of tattoos, swords, guns, baseball bats, ropes, scowls, leers, scars, rubber suits, school uniforms, cartoon characters, and half-naked women. Also includes Sci-Fi, Samurai, Anime and New Cinema.

ISBN 0-9723124-0-4

---

cocoro books

SECRETS OF THE NINJA

THEIR TRAINING,TOOLS AND TECHNIQUES

Now you see them, now you don't. Peek inside the Ninja's world and discover the skills, weapons, and ingenious tricks that made these men and women feared and revered for centuries. Learn Ninja techniques for meditation, stealth, and fighting dirty. Study their diet, ancient codes, workout and accupressure points. Find out what it really meant to be a Ninja in old Japan.

ISBN 0-9723124-1-2

cocoro books

Cosplay Girls

JAPAN'S LIVE ANIMATION HEROINES

Cosplay, the peculiarly Japanese hobby of making and wearing the outfits of manga, anime and video-game characters, is catching on fast overseas. *Cosplay Girls* introduces Japanese cosplay fans of manga, anime and games, from *Streetfighter* and *Samurai Spirits* to *Ranma 1/2* and *Urusei Yatsura.* It's also packed with info on the characters they portray, how to pose, and methods of making and wearing costumes. As well as a fun guide to games, manga and anime big in Japan, *Cosplay Girls* also highlights the creative powers of Japanese otaku girls.

ISBN 0-9723124-2-0